Hymns for the Drowning

Princeton Library
of Asian Translations

Hymns for the Drowning

Poems for Viṣṇu by Nammāḻvār

Translated from Tamil by
A. K. Ramanujan

PRINCETON UNIVERSITY PRESS
PRINCETON, NEW JERSEY

Published by Princeton University Press, Princeton, New Jersey
In the United Kingdom: Princeton University Press,
Guildford, Surrey

Library of Congress Cataloging in Publication Data will be found on the last printed page of this book

Publication of this book has been aided by a grant from the Paul Mellon Fund of Princeton University Press

This book has been composed in Linotron Bembo

Clothbound editions of Princeton University Press books are printed on acid-free paper, and binding materials are chosen for strength and durability

Printed in the United States of America by
Princeton University Press, Princeton, New Jersey

For Loraine and Cam

Contents

Introduction

The poems in this book are some of the earliest religious poems about Viṣṇu, or Tirumāl, the Dark One. The author is an āḻvār, "[one] immersed in god"; the root verb *āḻ* means "to immerse, to dive; to sink, to be lowered, to be deep." The title *Hymns for the Drowning* plays on the meanings of such an immersion for poet and reader.[1]

Tradition recognizes twelve āḻvārs, saint-poets devoted to Viṣṇu.[2] Between the sixth and the ninth century, in the Tamil-speaking region of South India, these devotees of Viṣṇu and their counterparts, the devotees of Śiva (nāyaṉmār), changed and revitalized Hinduism, and checked the spread of Buddhism and Jainism while absorbing some of the features of these rivals. The saint-poets wandered all over the Tamil countryside, inspiring and converting kings, brahmans, and peasants, affirming in poetry the holiness of hundreds of Tamil places dedicated to Viṣṇu or Śiva. Their pilgrimages, their legends, and their hymns (which they sang by the thousand) literally mapped a sacred

[1] Immersion in god, "who is the deep of deeps" appears as a metaphor in various traditions: Evelyn Underhill, *Mysticism*, p. 425. For another kind of drowning, see p. 84; also the common phrase *saṃsārasāgara* "the ocean of life-in-the-world."

[2] The twelve āḻvārs were Poykai, Pūtam, Pēy, Tiruppāṇ, Tirumaḻicai, Toṇṭaraṭippoṭi, Kulacēkaraṉ, Periyāḻvār, Āṇṭāḷ, Tirumaṅkai, Nammāḻvār and Maturakavi, in the order of their listing in the *Irāmānucanūṟṟantāti*, "the earliest and most authoritative work mentioning the Vaiṣṇava saints in chronological order." Kamil Zvelebil, *Tamil Literature*, pp. 155ff. Of these, the first three belong to the seventh century, the rest to the ninth. Zvelebil, *Tamil Literature*, pp. 155-62. To my knowledge, the traditional title *āḻvār* does not occur in the poems.

geography of the Tamil regions and fashioned a communal self-image that cut across class and caste. They composed the most important early bhakti (devotional) texts in any Indian language. The two rival movements, despite differences in myth and ritual, created and shared a special idiom, a stock of attitudes and themes, and a common heritage alive to this day. A new generation of scholars has become interested in the āḻvārs during the last ten years, but very little of the poetry is available in translation.[3]

The author of the poems in this book had several names, for example, Māṟaṉ and Caṭakōpaṉ, but he was best known as Nammāḻvār, "our own āḻvār." He is considered the greatest of the twelve āḻvārs. Anyone

[3] During the last decade, a number of books and Ph.D. dissertations have appeared in English on the āḻvārs: for instance, J. Filliozat, *Le Tiruppāvai d'Āṇṭāḷ*; A. Srinivasa Raghavan, *Nammalvar*; Friedhelm Hardy, "Emotional Kṛṣṇa bhakti" (which I have not been able to consult); Lynn M. Ate, "Periyāḻvār's 'Tirumoḻi'—a Bāla Kṛṣṇa Text from the Devotional Period in Tamil Literature"; K.K.A. Venkatachari, *The Maṇipravāla Literature of the Śrīvaiṣṇava Ācāryas, 12th to 15th Century A.D.*; Katherine Young, "Beloved Places (Ukantaruḷiṉanilaṅkaḷ): The Correlation of Topography and Theology in the Śrīvaiṣṇava Tradition of South India"; Vasudha Rajagopalan, "The Śrī Vaiṣṇava Understanding of Bhakti and Prapatti (from the āḻvārs to Vedānta Deśika)"; Norman Cutler, *Consider Our Vow* and "The Poetry of the Tamil Saints." F. Gros, trans., *Le Paripāṭal*, and John B. Carman, *The Theology of Rāmānuja, an Essay in Interreligious Understanding*, are also directly relevant. The best-known earlier translations of the āḻvārs are in J.S.M. Hooper, *Hymns of the Āḻvārs*; however, it contains no translations from Nammāḻvār's *Tiruvāymoḻi*. For recent and readable verse translations, see Raghavan (Nammāḻvār), Ate (Periyāḻvār), and Cutler (Poykai, Pūtam, Pēy, and Nammāḻvār selections). Kamil Zvelebil, *A History of Tamil Literature* and *Tamil Literature*, include literary and bibliographic discussions of the saints.

who reads his poems can see why: the poems are at once philosophic and poetic, direct in feeling yet intricate in design, single-minded yet various in mood—wondering, mischievous, tender, joyous, subtly probing, often touching despair but never staying with it. He composed four works, of which the 1,102 verses of *Tiruvāymoḻi* ("holy word of mouth"/"word of holy mouth"—"god-spell," if you wish), are the most important. Very early, the *Tiruvāymoḻi* was hailed as "the ocean of Tamil Veda in which the Upaniṣads of the thousand branches flow together."[4]

According to historians, Nammāḻvār was born into a peasant caste (veḷḷāḷa) and lived from approximately A.D. 880 to 930.[5] Some would date him a century earlier. Although the facts are hazy, the legends are vivid and worth retelling. According to these latter, he lived for only 35 years. He was born in Tirukurukūr (today's Āḻvārtirunakari, in Tamilnadu), into a princely family in answer to their penance and prayers. When he was born, the overjoyed mother gave him her breast but the child would have nothing of it. He uttered no

[4] The phrase occurs in the opening Sanskrit panegyric appended to the Tamil text.

[5] For the names, eulogies, and legends of Nammāḻvār, see Friedhelm Hardy, "The Tamil Veda of a Śūdra Saint," the best essay on the subject. The first full-length account occurs in *Garuḍavāhana*'s *Divyasūricaritam* (12th-13th century) and Pinpaḻakiya Perumāḷ Jīyar's *Guruparamparāprabhāvam* (13th century).

Veḷḷāḷas of the Coromondel plain must not be underestimated. Their "ubiquity and prestige . . . has been a marked feature of agrarian society until the present time." Burton Stein, "Brahman and Peasant in Early South Indian History," p. 242. Nammāḻvār often calls himself a *nāṭaṉ*, "belonging to a *nāṭu*"; *nāṭu* probably meant agricultural councils concerned with secular as well as temple affairs—councils that were comprised of all four castes. Hardy, "The Tamil Veda," pp. 32-33. For dates, see Zvelebil, *Tamil Literature*; Hardy prefers the 7th or early 8th century.

sound, sat if seated, lay if laid down, seemed both deaf and mute. The distressed parents left the child at the feet of a local Viṣṇu idol. Once there, he got to his feet, walked to a great tamarind tree, entered a hollow in it and sat like a yogi in a lotus posture, with his eyes shut and turned inward.

Meanwhile, in North India, Maturakavi, a pilgrim poet and scholar, was wandering near the Ganges; suddenly he saw a light in the southern sky. He watched it for three days and followed it all the way to Kurukūr, where, having led him to the silent child in the tamarind hollow, it vanished. Maturakavi tried in vain to wake the yogi by clapping his hands and dashing stones on the temple walls. Finally, he went to the hole in the tree and asked, "Master, if the subtle [spirit] is embodied in the gross [matter], what will it eat, where will it rest?" The yogi at once replied: "*That* it will eat, and *there* it will rest!" Maturakavi realized at once that God was what the Master ate, and God was what he lived in. With that exchange, master and disciple found each other; the master broke his life-long silence and poured forth more than a thousand hymns to Viṣṇu. The thousand magnificent hymns, each beginning with the last word of the previous one, were one continuous poem—an icon for the endless, ever-changing forms of the Lord.

Such was Nammāḻvār's fame and importance that, soon after his death, images of him were installed in South Indian Viṣṇu temples, and revered as the very feet of God. In these temples today every worshiper's head receives the touch of a special crown that represents Viṣṇu's feet and our āḻvār; it is named *caṭakōpam* after him. He is called the "first lord of our lineage." He is the "body," the other saints are the "limbs." His poems have been chanted in temple services and processions since the eleventh century. Indeed, at the Śrīraṅkam temple a special ten-day festival is devoted to his work: a professional reciter (with the title *araiyar*, "king"), dressed in ritual finery, sings and enacts the hymns for the listening image of Lord Viṣṇu.[6]

A certain Nātamuṉi (10th century?) gathered and ordered the compositions of the twelve Vaiṣṇava saints and arranged for their recitation. According to tradition, he heard visitors from Nammāḻvār's birthplace of Kurukūr recite ten stanzas, and he saw that they were only ten out of a thousand. So he went to Kurukūr, worshiped Viṣṇu, and meditated as a yogi, but he failed to invoke the poet or receive the poems. Then he recited 12,000 times Maturakavi's praise-poems about his master, Nammāḻvār. Both Maturakavi and Nammāḻvār appeared to him in a vision and gave him a knowledge of the āḻvār's four works. Some accounts say, he received all of the four thousand in this way. His grandson Yāmuna (10th-11th century), celebrated in Sanskrit the "impeccable [Tamil] scriptures" collected by Nātamuṉi. It is significant that both grandfather and grandson were priests at the Śrīraṅkam temple. Through them and through Rāmānuja (11th-12th century), a non-Sanskritic, non-brahmanical religious literature (Nammāḻvār was a śūdra saint) became central to brahman orthodoxy. Inscriptions as early as the 11th century mention endowments of land for the maintenance of reciters for the āḻvārs' hymns.

Nātamuṉi thus became the first link between the

[6] K. Gnanambal, "Srivaishnavas and Their Religious Institutions," pp. 126-27; V. N. Hari Rao, *Kōil Oḻugu, The Chronicle of the Śrīrangam Temple, with Historical Notes*, pp. 33-37. Reciters sing all the four thousand hymns in twenty-one days in Mārkaḻi month (December-January).

saint-poets and the Viṣṇu temples, between text and ritual; he was the first of a long line of teachers (*ācāryas*) who formed the theology and the institutions of the "Śrī Vaiṣṇava" sect.

His compilation was called "The Four Thousand Divine Compositions" (*Nālāyira Divyaprabandham*), shortened to the "Four Thousand" (*Nālāyiram*) or the "Divine Composition" (*Divyaprabandham*). Orthodox Śrī Vaiṣṇavas deemed the Four Thousand equal to the four Vedas. Sanskrit and Tamil, the Vedas and the Four Thousand, were integrated in their domestic and temple services. The singers of the Tamil hymns led the temple processions, walked before the god; and the Vedas followed behind.

These texts are not merely the living scripture of an important sect; they have attracted many subtle and brilliant commentators. The Four Thousand, particularly Nammāḻvār's thousand verses in the *Tiruvāymoḻi*, and the commentaries stand at the head of a philosophic genealogy of all Vaiṣṇava ideas, culminating in Rāmānuja's qualified monism or monism-with-a-difference (*viśiṣṭādvaita*).[7] As poems, they are the forebears of later traditions of Vaiṣṇava poetry, reaching as far as

[7] Rāmānuja (ca. 1050-1137) "refuted the doctrine of Māyā (the world as illusion) propounded by Śaṅkara (7th-8th century), demonstrated that the upanishads did not teach a strict monism, and built up the philosophy of Visishtādvaita which reconciled devotion to a personal God with . . . Vedanta by affirming that 'the soul though of the same substance as God and emitted from him rather than created, can obtain bliss not in absorption but in existence near him. . . .' Though he did not depart from the traditional caste organization of society, . . . he affirmed the universality of *bhakti* and the spiritual equality of the *bhaktas*. . . . He travelled all over India to spread his ideas and this may well have been the origin of the wide influence of his sect in North India." K. A. Nilakanta Sastri, *The Culture and History of the Tamils*, p. 116.

Caitanya in 16th-century Bengal and Tagore in our own times. Characteristic pan-Indian themes find some of their first and finest expressions in the poetry of the āḻvārs—themes such as the Lord's creation as play (*līlā*), Viṣṇu's incarnations, Kṛṣṇa's childhood, Lord and devotee as lover and beloved, to name only a few. A number of these themes and their relation to Hinduism at large are explored in the Afterword.

This book contains eighty-three poems; seventy-six of them are selected from the *Tiruvāymoḻi*, and seven, love-poems in the classical style, from the *Tiruviruttam*. My arrangement is as much a part of the "translation" as my verse. The original verses are arranged in tens, which are in turn arranged (by the compilers) in hundreds, following a long Tamil tradition.[8] Yet single verses have an existence of their own; they are quoted and recited as complete poems. Each group of ten is unified by meter, theme, and diction, but the transition from each group to the next is not always clear; commentators offer various schemes. I have taken the liberty of offering one of my own that, I think, also reflects the tradition. In doing so, I have sometimes brought together similar-looking poems from different parts of the original anthology, keeping in mind, and often playing on, an overarching rhythm of themes.

[8] Numbers like "ten," "hundred," and "thousand" (*pattu*, *nūṟu*, *āyiram*) should be treated usually as generic names for verse arrangements. For instance, each "ten" of the *Tiruvāymoḻi* consists really of eleven poems. The eleventh is a signature and a meta-poem, a *phalaśruti* or *śrutiphala* (a recital of results) describing the merits of the ten verses and the good results they will bring to the devoted reader or listener. The *Tiruvāymoḻi*, called the fourth "thousand," really consists of 1,102 poems: ninety-nine sets of ten, plus one irregular set of twelve (for the twelve names of Viṣṇu) adding up to 1,002 hymns, plus 100 phalaśruti verses.

For instance, I have cycles of love poems alternating with philosophic and other hymns, as in the original text. Such cycles and epicycles, with returning voices, roles, and places, are part of the "interinanimation" of these poems. I have placed ten poems on the works of Viṣṇu (his incarnations, etc.) at the beginning—for they weave into the allusive network of the other poems. My arrangement also enacts the progression: from wonder at the Lord's works, his play, his contrariety, to the experience of loving him and missing him, of watching others (one's friends, one's daughters) love him and suffer over him, to moods of questioning and despair, and on to an experience of being devoured, possessed, taken over, till the very poems that speak of him are of his own speaking.

To translate is to "carry across"; "metaphor" has the same root-meaning. Translations are transpositions; and some elements of the original cannot be transposed at all. For instance, one can often convey a sense of the original rhythm but not the language-bound meter; one can mimic levels of diction, even the word play, but not the actual sound of the words. Items are more difficult to translate than relations, textures more difficult than structure, words more difficult than phrasing, linear order more difficult than syntax, lines more difficult than pattern. Yet poetry is made at all those levels—and so is translation. The ideal is still Dryden's, "a kind of drawing after the life": ". . . to steer betwixt the two extremes of paraphrase and literal translation; to keep as near my author as I could, without losing all his graces, the most eminent of which are in the beauty of his words; and those words, I must add, are always figurative . . . taking all the materials of this divine author, I have endeavoured to make [him] speak such

English as he would himself have spoken . . . in this present age."[9]

When two languages are as startlingly different from each other as modern English and medieval Tamil, one despairs. For instance, the "left-branching" syntax of Tamil is most often a reverse mirror image of the possible English. Medieval Tamil is written with no punctuation and no spaces between words; it has neither articles nor prepositions, and the words are "agglutinative," layered with suffixes. Moreover, the syntax is a dense embedding of clause within clause. I translate unit by syntactic unit and try to recreate the way the parts articulate the poem in the original. My English thus seems to occupy more visual space on the page than the adjective-packed, participle-crowded Tamil original. The "sound-look," the syntax, the presence or absence of punctuation, and the sequential design are part of the effort to bring the Tamil poems faithfully to an English reader. The Notes and the Afterword are aimed at translating the reader toward the poems. I have consulted various texts and commentaries in learning to read these poems. Chief among these are: the ten volumes of Aṇṇaṅkarācāriyār and the ten of Purushottama Naidu. I have used the standard *Tamil Lexicon* system to transliterate Tamil words.

Many years ago, John Carman urged me to translate the āḻvārs. In 1976, in the subzero sun of a Minnesota winter, I read and reread the *Tiruvāymoḻi* with care, and these ancient poems came alive for me. My thanks are due to John Carman of Harvard, and to my friends at Carleton College, Northfield, Minnesota,—especially to Bardwell Smith, Eleanor Zelliott, and James Fisher.

[9] John Dryden, "The Dedication of the Aeneis."

Keith Harrison, poet and translator, read an entire earlier draft: his friendship has changed not only these poems. I also wish to thank Friedhelm Hardy, Vasudha Narayanan, Ronald Inden, James Lindholm, Wendy O'Flaherty, David Grene, Norman Cutler, Chirantan Kulasreshtha, and my wife Molly for criticism laced with kindness.

Chicago, 1980

Hymns for the Drowning

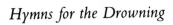

The Paradigm

We here and that man, this man,
  and that other in-between,
and that woman, this woman,
  and that other, whoever,

those people, and these,
  and these others in-between,
this thing, that thing,
  and this other in-between, whichever,

all things dying, these things,
  those things, those others in-between,
good things, bad things,
  things that were, that will be,

being all of them,
he stands there.

1.1.4

The Works of Viṣṇu—I

1 • HE PACES THE WORLDS

First, the discus
  rose to view,

then the conch,
        the long bow,
        the mace,
        and the sword;

with blessings
  from the eight quarters,

he broke through
  the egg-shell of heaven,
   making the waters bubble;

giant head and giant feet
  growing away from each other,

time itself rose to view:

how the lord
  paced and measured

all three worlds!

7.4.1

2 • CHURNING THE SEA

That moment:

with the sound
of rivers streaming backward
into their mountains

and the sound
of the serpent
wrapped around the mountain

and the sound
of the sea churning
now left now right

the lord
drew out the gods' elixir
that rose slowly in the churning

7.4.2

3 • THE BOAR RESCUES THE EARTH

No, they did not come apart:

the seven islands of the earth,
they stayed in place;

and the seven mountains,
they stayed in place;

and the seven seas
did not go wild
but stayed in place

miraculously,
            that day

our lord pitchforked them out
with his tusks
from the deep.

7.4.3

4 • A MEAL

Season
    day and hour
went out of kilter

so did earth
            water
        the planets and the skies

fire
  wind
    the mountains and the stars:

O what a roaring meal
      of chaos

our lord made
    of the seven worlds!

7.4.4

5 • THE EPIC WAR

When our lord managed
that spectacular Bhārata war,
what noises!

Noise of well-fed wrestlers
falling in combat,

the jitter
of whole armies
of regal men,

and the noises of the gods
jostling in heaven
to watch the fun!

7.4.5

6 • THE MAN-LION

At the red hour of sunset,
there was blood
on the heavens and the eight directions.

Our lord
plunged the demon into despair
and slaughtered him:

a lion
tearing open
a mountain under his claws.

7.4.6

7 • THE SACK OF LAṄKĀ

Crowding each other
face to face
as the arrows sang
and jangled

demon carcasses fell
in hundreds
rolled over
like hills

the sea stained with blood
backed upstream into the rivers

when our lord and father
ravaged the island

and left it
a heap of ash

7.4.7

8 • THE DEMON OF ARROWS

The cock-bannered young god
ran away

the inflamed god of fire
ran away

even three-eyed Śiva
ran

when our lord and father
tackled the fleeing Demon of Arrows

and broke his fat arms

7.4.8

9 • CREATION

In that original moment,
our lord and father

made earth, water, fire, wind,
                    and sky
        and the mountains;

made the two lights,
        sun and moon,
        and other such bodies;

then   the rain,
        and all that lives by rain,
        and the gods of rain.

In that moment,
he made the worlds
for the first time.

7.4.9

10 • KṚṢṆA LIFTS THE MOUNTAIN

The grazing cows tumble,
    the animals turn over,

the water in the mountain pools
    rushes down in waterfalls,

as our lord and father
lifts up the mountain

so his rich city,
    his City of Gateways,

might take shelter
against the downpour
    of heaven's evils.

7.4.10

My "Quite Contrary" Lord

1

My lord
  who's both dearth and plenty
    hell and heaven
    friendship
        enmity
    venom and sweet ambrosia

my ranging various lord:

I saw him there
    in Viṇṇakar
        city named Sky
        city of rich houses

6.3.1

2

He is both the crooked
  and the straight

the black
        the white
the truths
      the lies

youth and age
  the ancient and the new:

our lord lives
  in Viṇṇakar
        strong-walled well-made city

and his grove there
  is the triple world
            of the gods

6.3.5

3

Being all three worlds
  and nothing

being desire
  being rage
being both the flower-born Lakṣmī
  and anti-Lakṣmī
    black goddess of ill luck

being both honor and shame

our lord
  lives in Viṇṇakar
            city named Sky
which the gods worship lovingly

and in my evil heart
he lives forever
      flame of flames

6.3.6

The Lord at Play

1

Worker of miracles,
  magical dwarf,
    and killer of the demon
        named Honey,

only you can tell us:

becoming fire, water, earth,
 sky, and wind,

becoming father, mother,
 and the children too
 and all others
 and all things unnamed,

the way you stand there,
 being yourself—

what's it all about?

7.8.1

2

O lord unending
wearing honey flowers
and basil leaf
in your hair

tell us this:

as moon
as sun
as the amazing numberless stars

as darkness
and as torrents of rain

as honor
as shame

and as death
with his cruel eyes

how fantastic
can you get?

7.8.2

3

You do stunts
  with your chariots

the discus your weapon:

tell us how

  managing every one of the four ages
  becoming every little thing in them

    harmonious now
      now quite contrary

you stand there

a marvel
 of contradictions!

7.8.3

4

Dwarf,
  you confuse everyone.

But make me understand:

becoming oblivion, memory,
  heat, cold,
  all things wonderful,
   and wonder itself,

becoming every act of success,
  every act of good and evil,
   and every consequence,

becoming even the weariness
  of lives,

you stand there—

and what misery you bring!

7.8.6

5

You dwell in heaven
 stand on the sacred mountain
 sleep on the ocean
 roll around in the earth

yet hidden everywhere
 you grow
 invisibly:

moving within
 numberless outer worlds

playing within my heart
 yet not showing your body

will you always play hide and seek?

6.9.5

Love Poems: The Playboy

1

Don't tell us those lies,

heaven and earth
 know your tricks.

Just one thing,
 my lord of the ancient wheel
  that turns at your slightest wish:

while all those girls
—their words pure honey—
stand there
wilting for love of you,

don't playact here and sweet-talk
 our lisping mynahs,
 our chattering parrots!

6.2.5

2

Look here:

being naughty,
grabbing our dolls
and doing wild things

won't get you anywhere;

we know you
from old times,
how can we stand your pranks,
your airs?

There are any number
of lovely women,
queens of the three worlds;

so don't torment
this plain crowd.

Such stuff is childish,
even for you.

6.2.6

3

Pure one,
  you devoured once
    the sea-surrounded world.

Great one,
  it isn't right to grab
    our dolls and toys.

What's wrong is wrong
    even for you.

You tease us with sweet talk:
if my brothers hear of it,

they won't wait to see
  right and wrong,
they'll just bring out
    their sticks

and beat you up.

6.2.7

4

Rich and perfect sound
  of strings
  on an ancient lute

other than all others
  that good men study

purity
  sweetness of sugarcane
        and ambrosia

O dark raincloud
    Kṛṣṇa

without you
  I'm not:

take me

2.3.6

Questions

1

Suppose I have the three worlds
or even better
 I become all of myself
  as I could
   only in heaven

would it ever be
 like the goodness
    the pleasure I feel
  right here in this world

when I worship at the feet
 of his men
  who work at his feet

    his body dark as thundercloud
    feet covered with flowers
     and anklets of war?

8.10.2

2

Would I, sinner that I am,
rather enter the fragrance,
the lotus feet
of our lord,

divine dwarf
making great his little body
till it overwhelms
all three worlds,

when my masters,
his great servants
who have taken on small
human lives,

are content to roam this world?

8.10.3

3

Where shall I reach you?

You are the three worlds
in all their beauty

you are the three-eyed one
the four-faced god
and the rain king
brandishing the lightning axe
of diamond

and you are other gods as well

my lord
my cowherd
cool flowers and fragrant basil
in your hair

just where shall I reach you?

7.6.4

4

My cowherd
  my rough dark diamond

how will this self of mine
  ever-trammeled in the three
   worlds unfolding
        in your navel's lotus

how will it come through
  and reach you there

in your overwhelming world of light?

7.6.5

5

Feet, navel, hands,
  chest, eyes, and lips

red-rayed jewels
  set in a blue glow,

and golden silks round his waist,

my lord is all blaze and dazzle:
I do not know how to reach him.

7.6.6

6

Shedding pleasure
            displeasure
 birth   illness
  age
   and death

when will I join
        lit like a flame

those congregations
 of my lord of illusions

   my lord
     who shelters the raining sky
     and this earth
   with his conch shell and wheel of fire?

2.3.10

7

Only men who live by the Vedas qualify,
  can wear your feet on their heads,
          lord
          of blue-black body
          and eyes like lotuses,

but, you know, when the town's cattle moo
coming home,
the blind one moos too:

so I too speak of you,
how else?

Tiruviruttam 94

Love Poems: The Dark One

1

What She Said

Evening has come,
  but not the Dark One.

The bulls,
  their bells jingling,
  have mated with the cows
and the cows are frisky.

The flutes play cruel songs,
  bees flutter in their bright
        white jasmine
  and the blue-black lily.

The sea leaps into the sky
        and cries aloud.

Without him here,
  what shall I say?
  how shall I survive?

9.9.10

2

What She Said

Our Kaṇṇan dark as rain cloud
has stolen my heart
and it has gone away with him
all by itself.

But this north wind
seems ready for battle.

Gathering the sweet smoke of incense,
the beauty of lutestrings,
the fifth tune of night and love,
and cool moist sandal

it blows and blows,
culling on its way
the fragrance of new jasmine,

and it burns:

how can I say anything to anyone
O mothers?

9.9.7

3

What Her Mother Said

O women,
    you too have daughters
    and have brought them up.

    How can I tell you
    about my poor girl?

    She talks of the conch shell,
    she talks of the wheel,
    and she talks, night and day,
      of the basil in his hair,

what shall I do?

4.2.9

4

What Her Mother Said

When she sees kings,
she says, I see my lord.

When she sees shapes and colors,
she leaps up, saying,
I see him who measured the world.

All temples with gods in their wombs
are, she says, places of the lord dark as the sea.

In terror, in love, in every mood,
she wants
the Dark One's anklets.

4.4.7

Waxing and Waning

1

These five senses—
  they run into the ground
          even the men
          who serve the great lord of heaven—

if they get me
and if you too
    let go of me
what will they not do?

Lord of all
  you already know my song
                    my poem
                      my feeling

indweller of eyes
 O inward of my heart
          my words

come
say something

7.1.6

2

My head
is the hill
of the lord's gardens
the ocean of milk

my body
the paradisal dwelling-place of Viṣṇu
Vēṅkaṭam hill
cool and holy:

O breath of life
endlessly tangled in illusion

heart
word
all my many acts

he will not leave you
not one fraction
of one second

the one
the only one

first person of all time

10.7.8

3

It's true
even I am you

even the unbearable hell
    of this world
 is you:

 this being so
  what's the difference?

One may go to paradise
    and reach perfect joy
or go the other way
   and fall into hell

yet I being I
   even when I remember
 I am you
I still fear hell:

lord in perpetual paradise
let me be at your feet.

8.1.9

4

For the sake of that girl,
her mouth red as a berry,
you broke the seven bulls;

you bent the long bow
and finished off the king
of the island of towers;

and you broke the tusk
of that pedigreed elephant.

I haven't worshiped you
with flowers and holy water
at proper times;

but then
my heart is the only sandalwood
to rub and perfume your body with,

your body
dark as *kāyā* blossom.

4.3.1

5

He is
for he cannot *not* be
for his men

for others he is
as if he is not

our lord
is here
he lives here in me

and we're done with
growing and perishing
waxing and waning
like the moon—

done with
knowing
and unknowing
like sunshine and nightdark

8.8.10

6

You're what they said
in the Good Old Books:
"Than this
there's nothing more subtle"

you are that form
and that formlessness

everlasting
you wear lotus and basil
on your chest

and whenever we say
whatever we can
it becomes you

however we say it

7.8.10

7

Lotus-eyed,
 he is in my eyes.

I see him now,
 for his eyes cleanse my sight;

and all five senses
 are his bodies.

Making possible
 a brahmā in the lotus
 and a śiva with an eye
 in his forehead,

making the purest gods
 and the many worlds,

he is right here
 in my brow.

1.9.9

Love Poems: You Too?

1

Since the time
  time began

bringing water to the world

melting like me
    and my girlfriends here

O sky

are you stricken too
  by my lord
    enemy of the demon
      named Honey?

are you also
  bless you
 perishing for love of him?

2.1.5

2

One-day moon:
  are you languishing too
   like us

with no strength
  to drive away the dark today,

faint
 and shrinking,

jilted by the true-seeming words
 of our lord
   fast asleep
     on the five-headed serpent,

our lord of the mighty wheel,

have you also lost
  the natural light of your body?

2.1.6

3

You roam the seas,
  the mountains, the skies,
you touch them lightly,

cold north wind!

Night and day,
  lit by alternate lamps
    of sun and moon,
like us
you wander sleepless:

are you also craving,
since the time
  time began,

for a glimpse
  of our lord of the mighty wheel?

2.1.4

The Works of Viṣṇu—II

1 • BY RĀMA'S GRACE

Why would anyone want
to learn anything but Rāma?

Beginning with the low grass
and the creeping ant
with nothing
whatever,

he took everything in his city,
everything moving,
everything still,

he took everything,
everything born
of the lord
of four faces,

he took them all
to the very best of states.

7.5.1

2 • THE DWARF

When I didn't know a thing
you made me love
your service

mixing inseparably
with my soul

when I
your servant
was in the illusion of unknowing:

you dwarf incognito
who once said to great Bali
"Give me space
just three steps"

and cheated him of everything
before anyone knew

2.3.3

3 • BEFORE I COULD SAY

Before I could say,
    "He became cowherd
        fish
         wild boar,"
he became a million million.

1.8.8

4 • HE AND I

He who took the seven bulls
    by the horns
  he who devoured the seven worlds

made me his own cool place
    in heaven

and thought of me
    what I thought of him

and became my own thoughts

1.8.7

5

Three loves never part from him—
Lakṣmī, goddess of all good things,
the Earth,
and the simple cowherd girl.

Ruling three worlds,
devouring them altogether,
my lord rests on a banyan leaf:

darker than the sea,
Kaṇṇan,
child perching on my hip.

1.9.4

Love's Messengers

1

Is that you, little bird?

When I asked you to go
  as my messenger to the great lord
  and tell him of my pain,

you dawdled, didn't go.

I've lost my looks,
 my dark limbs are pale.

Go look for someone else
  to put sweet things
  in your beak,
  go now.

1.4.8

2

The cold wind threads through my bones.

Remembering only my faults,
my lord doesn't show me any grace.
Go ask him,
                "What wrong did she do?"

Dear parrot gnawing at a bone,
  please, go ask him.

I brought you up, didn't I?

1.4.7

Idiots, Monists, and Others

1 • GOD'S IDIOTS

Mumbling and prattling
        the many names
            of our lord of the hill
with cool waterfalls,
    long strands of water,

while onlookers say,
    "They're crazy,"

entering and not entering
    cities,
standing still or swaying
    before a laughing world,

they dance, they leap,
    undone by feeling—

and the gods bow down
    before them.

3.5.8

2

Master
of illusions

with no one equal
or above

form and breath of all things:

becoming mother and father
you made me know
what I couldn't know

I do not even know
the things you've done for me

2.3.2

If they should merge,
that's really good:

if the two that'll never meet
should meet,
then this human thing
will become our lord,
the Dark One
with the sacred bird
on his banner—
as if that's possible.

It will always be itself.

There are yogis
who mistake fantasy
for true release

and run around
in circles
in the world
of what is and what was
and what will be.

It takes all kinds.

8.8.9

You believers in Liṅga mythologies
and you Jainas
you Buddhists

becoming all of you choppers of logic
becoming even your gods

he stands there
our lord:

come see him in Kurukūr
where rich ears of paddy
fan him like ceremonial yak-tails.

In this place without lies
come praise him.

4.10.5

No More Kings

1

My lord of a thousand names
  gives and gives

the fame of his giving
 crosses all boundaries

I cannot praise anyone else
 cannot say to some paltry thing
  of this world:

  "Your hand is bounteous as the rain
  your shoulders are strong as the mountains"

I cannot tell such barefaced lies

3.9.7

2

Kings
  who rule the earth all alone
  for long years

will one day hobble
on legs bitten by black dogs

and beg from a broken pot
here
  in this very life
with the whole world watching:

don't tarry then

think of the lord's feet
and live

4.1.1

3 • OUR MASTERS

The four castes
   uphold all clans;
go down, far down
   to the lowliest outcastes
      of outcastes:

if they are the intimate henchmen
  of our lord
    with the wheel in his right hand,
    his body dark as blue sapphire,

then even the slaves of their slaves
      are our masters.

3.7.9

Love Poems: Four Returning Voices

1

What She Said

Making the earth shiver,
crowding and wetting the world
with their waters,
scratching with their hooves,

the dark blue bulls of heaven
fight with each other.

And I,
doing good and evil,
cannot tell what's before me:

is it or is it not
the cold monsoon
bearing the shape
of my dark lord,

speaking of his cruelty,
his going away?

Tiruviruttam 7

2

What He Said

The sight I see now
is rare indeed.

Even as I say, "Dear girl,
   dear as our Dark One's paradise,
I've got to go away and far away
to get rich,"

her eyes
bring enough to buy a world,

eyes,
   each large as the palm of a hand,
   shaped like a carp,
dropping pearls
and grief yellow as gold.

Tiruviruttam 11

3

What She Said

Skin dark as young mango leaf
      is wilting.
Yellow patches spread all over me.
Night is as long as several lives.

All these are the singular dowry
my good heart brings
as she goes over

  to the cool basil
  of my lord, the Dark One
with the wheel that cuts down demons.

Tiruviruttam 12

4

What She Said to Her Girlfriend

Dear friend,
  dear as the Dark One's paradise,

night grows long, many lives long,
    when we part;
or goes fast, a split second many times split,
    when we are together.

So I suffer even when my lover joins me
    many nights in a row,
and suffer again
    when he goes away.

Blessed night, ever flowing,
  is full of tricks,
  plays fast and loose.

Tiruviruttam 16

5

What Her Foster Mother Said

She's young:
breasts not even full-grown;
hair thick, soft, but much too short;
her dress doesn't cover her waist
and her tongue stammers;

but her eyes,
so priceless
earth and sea cannot buy them,
they flash everywhere.

She's learning to say,
"Is Vēṅkaṭam
the hill of our Lord?"

Will she ever get there?

Tiruviruttam 60

6

What Her Girlfriend Said

They haven't flowered yet,
the fat *ko̲n̲r̲ai* trees,
nor hung out their garlands
    and golden circlets
in their sensual canopy of leaves
along the branches,

dear girl,
dear as the paradise of our lord
who measured the earth
    girdled by the restless sea,

they are waiting
with buds
for the return
of your lover
    once twined in your arms.

Tiruviruttam 68

My Lord, My Cannibal

1

My dark one
stands there as if nothing's
changed

after taking entire
into his maw
all three worlds
the gods
and the good kings
who hold their lands
as a mother would
a child in her womb—

and I
by his leave
have taken him entire

and I have him in my belly
for keeps

8.7.9

2

I don't understand why,

while all the worlds
live within him

and he lives within them
by birthright,

our lord of Kāṭkarai,
of gardens blowing with fragrance,

should assault
and devour this poor little
soul of mine

with his grace.

9.6.4

3

While I was waiting eagerly for him
saying to myself,

"If I see you anywhere
I'll gather you
and eat you up,"

he beat me to it
and devoured me entire,

my lord dark as raincloud,
my lord self-seeking and unfair.

9.6.10

Love Poems: A Case of Possession

1

"I made the world
    surrounded by the sea," says she.

"I became the world
    surrounded by the sea," says she.

"I once redeemed from the demon
    the world surrounded by the sea," says she.

"I pitchforked with my tusks
    the world once drowned in the sea," says she.

"I devoured once
    the world surrounded by the sea," says she.

Such talk!

Can it be because our lord
    of the world surrounded by the sea
has come and taken her over?

How can I explain
    my girl who lives within this world
        surrounded by the sea

to you people of this world
  surrounded by the sea?

5.6.1

2

My girl, who's just learning to speak
says,
"I'm beyond all learning.
I'm all the learning you learn."

"I'm the cause of all learning,
I end all learning,
I'm the essence of all learning,"
says she.

Does my girl talk this way
because our lord of all learning
has come and taken her over?

How can I tell you,
O learned men!

5.6.2

3

"I'm the earth you see," she says.

"I'm all the visible skies," she says.

"I'm the fires,
    the winds,
    and the seas," she says.

Is it because our lord dark as the sea
  has entered her and taken her over?

How can I explain my girl
    to you who see nothing
      but this world?

5.6.3

4

"I'm all that's being done," says she;

"all acts yet to be
    and all past acts," says she.

"I eat the fruit
    of all acts," says she,

"and make all others act."

Why does she act like this?

Is it because our lord with the lotus eyes
  has taken her over?

How can I explain
                our girl,

                    her lips red as a fruit,
                    her body lithe as a doe's,

how can I,
    to you innocents
    of this world?

5.6.4

5

My daughter says,
"Unfailing, I guard the earth."
"Unfailing, I lifted the mountain," says she,
"slew the demons,
taught strategems to the Five Brothers
once upon a time."
"Unfailing, I churned the ocean," says she.

Can it be that the unfailing lord,
his body dark as the sea,
has taken her over?
Good words fail
with my daughter now,
how can I tell you,
successful men of the world?

5.6.5

6

My little girl says,
"I've no relatives here
and everyone here is my relative."

"I'm the one who makes relatives relate,"
she says.

"I also end relations,
and to those related to me
I become all relations,"
she says.

Can it be the lord of illusions
beyond all relations
has come and taken her over?

How can I tell you,
my kinsmen,
what she means?

5.6.7

The Takeover

1

Poets,
  beware, your life is in danger:

the lord of gardens is a thief,
        a cheat,
  master of illusions;

he came to me,
  a wizard with words,
 sneaked into my body,
          my breath,

with bystanders looking on
      but seeing nothing,
  he consumed me
      life and limb,

and filled me,
        made me over
  into himself.

10.7.1

2

Becoming himself
  filling and becoming all worlds
    all lives
becoming him
  who becomes even me

singing himself
 becoming for my sake
  honey milk sugarcane
    ambrosia

becoming the lord of gardens too
  he stands there

 consuming me

10.7.2

3

I just said,
  "The grove and hill of my lord,"

and he came down
   and filled my heart;

he usually lives
  in the city of names

south of the Kāvēri,
  river of diamonds.

10.8.1

4

My lord
who lives in the city
of names
came here today

said he'd never leave
entered me
filled my heart

I've caught him
the big-bellied one
not content yet
with all that guzzling
on the sevenfold clouds
the seven seas
the seven mountains
and the world that holds them all

I've caught him
I contain him now

10.8.2

5

Promising me heaven,
making a pact with me,

today he entered this nest,
this thing of flesh,

himself cleared away
all obstacles
to himself,
all contrary acts,

our lord of the good city
of names,
whose groves are humming with bees.

10.8.5

6

Instead of getting his praises
sung by the great poets

he
comes here today,
gently

makes me over into himself
and gets me to sing of him,

my lord of paradise.

7.9.6

7

He who devoured all seven worlds
    happily came
   and entered me
and he will not leave now;

from now on
 what's not possible
       for me?

At one stroke
  seven generations below
   and seven above
have cleared a wilderness
              of trouble,

and escaped hell,
      hot, endless hell.

2.6.7

8

Even as I said,
"He became the master,
took me as servant,"
he came to me happily,
all grace,

my lord who became fish,
tortoise, man-lion, dwarf, wild boar,
and who'll soon be Kalki,

occupied me, became all of me,
my lord dark as raincloud.

5.1.10

9

A ship drowning,
calling out for help
in a lashing sea,

I tossed in this ocean of births
when the lord
        in his splendor,
        bearing wheel and conch,
called out to me: "O, O, you there!"

showed me his grace,
and became one with me.

5.1.9

10

My lord
who swept me away forever
into joy that day,

made me over into himself

and sang in Tamil
his own songs
through me:

what shall I say
to the first of things,
flame
standing there,

what shall I say
to stop?

7.9.1

Notes to the Poems

The Paradigm

For the Tamil original, and for an analysis, see Afterword, p. 122. The number 1.1.4 indicates that the verse is the fourth in the first decad of the first hundred verses. verses.

The Works of Viṣṇu—I

This decad of poems celebrates episodes in Viṣṇu mythology—chiefly the supremacy of Viṣṇu and his prowess. See Cornelia Dimmitt and J.A.B. van Buitenen, *Classical Hindu Mythology, a Reader in the Sanskrit Purāṇas*, pp. 59-98, for succinct translations of the major myths. A later group, "The Works of Viṣṇu—II," pp. 45-49, celebrates his grace and accessibility. Generally, I refer to the gods by their familiar Sanskritic names, for example, Viṣṇu, not Tirumāl.

Page 4. The poem describes Viṣṇu and one of his works: how, as Vāmana, he measured the worlds. Viṣṇu appeared as a dwarf, Vāmana, before the demon king Bali who once ruled the world. The dwarf asked for a gift of a piece of earth three paces wide. Generous Bali gave him the gift. At once Vāmana grew into gigantic Trivikrama, giant head and giant feet growing away from each other. He measured all earth in one stride, all heaven in another, and asked Bali where he could place his foot next. Bali, who saw that this figure was no other than Viṣṇu, bowed to him and asked him to place his foot on his (Bali's) head. Viṣṇu did so, and sent him to the netherworld. The name "Viṣṇu" means, "expander, pervader"; the Trivikrama figure is probably also symbolic of the sun traversing the heavens. The āḻvārs refer to the dwarf incarnation many times in their works. The co-presence of great and little, the outgrowth of the great from the small, obviously appeals to them. "By far the most important Vedic myth of Viṣṇu is the story of his three steps, a creation myth based upon the Vedic concept that to measure out, to spread, and to prop apart the elements of the universe is to create." Wendy Doniger O'Flaherty, *Hindu Myths*, p. 175.

Page 5. The gods and the antigods (*asuras*, often called "demons") churned the primal ocean. The king of serpents was the rope; the mountain Mandara was the churning rod. Viṣṇu, lord of the waters, became a tortoise so that the mountain could rest on his back. Out of the churning came the divine horse, the divine elephant, the goddess Lakṣmī, the moon, etc., which were distributed among the great gods, Indra, Śiva, and Viṣṇu. Finally, out of the sea rose a world-destroying poison. Śiva saved the world by drinking it at once; Pārvatī gripped him by the throat—so the poison stayed there, giving him the name "the poison-throated one." At last the elixir of the gods, *aṃṛta*, ambrosia, drink of immortality, rose from the sea. Viṣṇu took the form of a beautiful woman, Mohinī, bewitched the antigods, and distributed *aṃṛta* to all the gods, thus making them immortal. Thus began the division between the gods and the antigods, which motivates much of Hindu mythology. See O'Flaherty, *Hindu Myths*, p. 273 for details.

Page 6. Demon Hiraṇyākṣa abducted the earth and kept it under the ocean. Viṣṇu (in his third incarnation) became a boar, slew the demon after a thousand-year war, and lifted the earth from the waters with his tusks.

Page 7. During a deluge, the creator of worlds swallowed them all and protected them. See the use of this motif in 9.6.4, p. 68.

Page 8. The war scene in the *Mahābhārata* epic, with all the gods as onlookers. Viṣṇu as Kṛṣṇa is seen as the stage manager of the entire war. Note the playful, personal, eyewitness account of the myths.

Page 9. Hiraṇyakaśipu, a king of the antigods, received a boon from Brahmā that he should not be killed by weapons, thunderbolts, water, or fire; or by gods, demons, seers, and other creatures created by Brahmā; or in heaven, in earth, during the day or at night; neither from above, nor below. Viṣṇu took the form of a man-lion (Narasiṁha), who was neither man nor beast; took him on his knees—which was neither above nor below; at sunset—which was neither day nor night; and disemboweled the demon with his claws—which were not weapons; on a threshold—which was neither inside nor out.

Page 10. This poem pictures a war scene from the life of Rāma, who sacked the island of Laṅkā, and set fire to it.

Page 11. A reference to Bāṇāsura ("demon of arrows"), thousand-armed son of Bali, friend of Śiva, and enemy of Viṣṇu. His daughter, in love with Kṛṣṇa's grandson (Aniruddha), kidnapped him by magic. Kṛṣṇa, with his brother and son, fought with Bāṇa, who had Śiva and Skanda on his side. All three were routed by Kṛṣṇa. The cock-bannered young god is Murukaṉ (Skanda in

Sanskrit), with whom Viṣṇu-Tirumāl shares the distinction of being mentioned in the earliest Tamil bhakti poems, *Paripāṭal* and *Tirumurukāṟṟuppaṭai* ("A Guide to Lord Murukaṉ"), ca. 5th-6th century. Characteristically, this Vaiṣṇava poem praises Viṣṇu as more valiant than Murukaṉ or Śiva. Poems on the latter gods would subordinate Viṣṇu.

Page 12. 7.4.9 describes creation ending with rain. The *Tirukkuṟaḷ* (3rd-4th century?), the Tamil book for all occasions, after devoting its first ten verses to god, praises rain in ten more: Rain is the source of food, work, morale, and morality; without it, the sea will ebb, the gods will receive no worship.

> Rain ruins men; rain also lifts
> men out of ruin.
> *Tirukkuṟaḷ* 2.5

In Tamil poetry, the raincloud is an image of generosity; the rainy season is the time of the lover's return. The raincloud is also Kṛṣṇa, "the Dark One." Indra is the Vedic god of rain with lightning for his diamond weapon. See the next poem for Kṛṣṇa's supremacy over the rain god.

Page 13. The mountain is Govardhana. Kṛṣṇa persuaded the cowherds to make their offerings to the mountain instead of to Indra. Indra was furious and pelted the cows and cowherds with thunder and rain. Kṛṣṇa playfully lifted the mountain with one hand, and gave shelter to all the cows and cowherds for seven days and nights.

Dvārakā, Kṛṣṇa's city, means "place of gateways or doors [dvāra]"; the Tamils translate it literally as *vāyilpāṭi*. I follow their example in my English. Here and elsewhere, I translate proper names, for the original meanings are quite alive in the poems.

My "Quite Contrary" Lord

Page 14. The lord is characterized my *muraṇ*, "contrariety." Although all of him is auspicious, he informs both good and evil. The lord of all things and beyond is also here in Viṇṇakar, literally "sky-city" (a shrine in Tamilnadu), one of the 108 holy places. The āḻvārs (as interpreted by later theologians) saw god in three forms: *avatāra* "descent, incarnation," *antaryāmī* "inward controller," *arca* "the worshipable form" in a holy place. The three are continuous with each other, express different aspects of the divine.

Page 16. Lakṣmī, consort of Viṣṇu, goddess of good luck and beauty, and a-Lakṣmī, her elder sister and opposite. A-Lakṣmī, here translated as "anti-Lakṣmī," is called Mūtēvi ("the older goddess") and Jyēṣṭhā ("the elder sister")—both terms of abuse in Tamil.

The Lord at Play

Page 17. Sanskrit *līlā*, "sport, play, prank," Tamil *tiruviḷaiyāṭal*, "divine games," an aspect of the lord's mystery and the world's drama. In this view, not purpose but playfulness explains the one becoming many, the dualities of good and evil. Myth, eschatology, and personal questioning are fused in these poems. Madhu ("honey") and Kaiṭabha were demons who sprang from the ear of Viṣṇu, asleep at the end of an aeon; they went to attack Brahmā, the creator, born out of

Viṣṇu's navel lotus. Viṣṇu woke up in time and slew them. Therefore, one of his names is Madhusūdana ("killer of Madhu"). Such epithets are single-phrase summaries of his many acts; to recite them is to remember his entire history.

Page 18. Sanskrit *tuḷasī*, Tamil *tuḻāy*, Latin *ocymum sanctum*, the fragrant basil leaf is sacred to Vaiṣṇavas, who use it in their *pūjā* (worship) and consider it a transformed consort of the god. In this poem, as in many others, an eternal "unending" god is given attributes that are iconic (the basil), natural/cosmic (sun, moon), and social/psychological (honor, shame).

Page 19. Viṣṇu, the warrior-god, and here a chariot-driver. He plays charioteer to Arjuna in the *Mahābhārata*; hence his name "Pārthasārathī" ("charioteer to Pārtha, Arjuna"). The discus, or the wheel, is the god's favorite weapon and is named "Sudarśana." Viṣṇu obtains it as a boon from Śiva after standing on his big toe for an entire millennium. "A weapon that destroys all other weapons," it "resembles the wheel of time," with twelve spokes (months), six naves (seasons), etc. Dimmitt and van Buitenen, p. 92.

Page 20. Dwarf: Vāmana. See earlier note on 7.4.1 (p. 4). In this poem, Viṣṇu is both *karma* (which I translate as "acts of good and evil") and its fruit (*karmaphala*) or consequence. Later bhakti, and even Nammāḻvār elsewhere, pits the grace of god against *karma*. Bhakti is enjoined as an answer to *karma*. See A. K. Ramanujan, *Speaking of Śiva*, p. 36.

Love Poems: The Playboy

Page 22. Here are some of the earliest love poems written to Viṣṇu, especially in his Kṛṣṇa form. He is still Viṣṇu, with his "ancient wheel"; yet he has the character of a naughty playboy. The Kṛṣṇa figure appears early in Tamil poetry as Māyōn or Māl, the Dark One, god of the pastoral *mullai* landscape, then in the epic *Cilappatikāram* (Canto 17) in the milkmaids' songs, and in *Paripāṭal.* (See Kamil Zvelebil, "The Beginnings of Bhakti in South India," for a collation of references.) But it is in the āḻvārs' poems that he figures as a full-fledged god-lover. Probably, the Tamil tradition was incorporated into the Sanskrit *Bhāgavatapurāṇa* (10th century) and transmitted to other parts of India. See J.A.B. van Buitenen, "On the Archaism of the *Bhāgavata Purāṇa.*" For a discussion of Nammāḻvār's love poems, see Afterword, pp. 152-157.

Questions

Page 26. Afterword, pp. 143-146.

Page 27. An effective contrast between the little dwarf becoming great, and the great masters taking on little lives. In a way, the masters imitate the original act of the lord himself when he took on the form of the dwarf.

Page 28. Śiva is the three-eyed one, Brahmā the four-faced, Indra is the rain king. The poem begins with the great god and ends with the local cowherd.

Page 29. The dark-skinned body of Kṛṣṇa is contrasted with his dazzle. "Rough diamond" is a description of Viṣṇu in these poems and of Śiva in the contemporary Śaiva poems.

Page 32. The poem makes the āḻvār a cow; even a simple, transparent poem like this is laden with mythic associations. One name for Kṛṣṇa is Govinda "cowfinder," and his place is Gokula, "family/place of cows."

"We are told (in *Harivaṃśa* II: 19:30) that above manuṣyaloka (the world of men) is devaloka (the world of the gods), above that is Brahmaloka (the world of Brahmins) and even above that is the highest region, Goloka (the world of cattle), beyond which there is no region." Sukumari Bhattacharji, *The Indian Theogony: A Comparative Study of Indian Mythology from the Vedas to the Purāṇas*, pp. 309-310.

Love Poems: The Dark One

Page 33. The Dark One is Māyōṉ, dark herdsman god of the *mullai* or pastoral region, one of the five landscapes of classical Tamil; Māyōṉ is Kṛṣṇa.

Page 34. Kaṇṇaṉ is Tamil for Kṛṣṇa. North wind, perfume, lute music, sandal, and jasmine are all properties of a love scene and are aphrodisiac. In the absence of the lover, they are unbearable.

Pages 35-36. The āḻvār plays many parts in the mythic scenario—he is a girl in love with Viṣṇu, he is also her mother and her girlfriend. Here he is mother to his own love-sick heart. These personae are part of the repertoire of classical Tamil love poetry. See also the poems on pp. 52-53 and on pp. 70-75.

Waxing and Waning

Page 37. This set of poems describes the waxing and waning of one's intimacy with the lord.

Page 38. The "lord's gardens" is a holy place called Tirumāliruñcōlai, "the grove or garden where the Dark Lord dwells." The paradisal dwelling-place of Viṣṇu is *Vaikunṭha*, sometimes described as a place on Mt. Meru. Vēṅkaṭam hill (Tirupati) is, like Tirumāliruñcōlai, one of the 108 holy places celebrated by the āḻvārs.

Note how the poem moves from earthly holy places (Vēṅkaṭam) to mythic ones (oceans of milk) to parts of the body and parts of the devotee's own life-space (word, acts), and makes them continuous and analogous with each other.

Page 40. The first three sentences allude to three different acts of Viṣṇu/Kṛṣṇa: 1. Kṛṣṇa defeats seven bulls for the sake of a simple cowherd girl, Piṉṉai. 2. Rāma bends the long bow (called Śiva's Bow) in a contest of strength, wins his bride Sītā, who is abducted by Rāvaṇa to his island Laṅkā, which leads to Rāma's siege and destruction of the island. 3. Kaṃsa (the Herod-figure in the Kṛṣṇa story) sends a demon in elephant form (Kuvalayapīḍa) to trample Kṛṣṇa and his brother Balarāma to death—but the elephant is slain instead.

Kāyā is the bilberry, with dark purple flowers, *Memcylon tinctorium.*

Love Poems: You Too?

Pages 44-46. These three poems (examples of a genre) impute the pangs of love to the elements and make common cause with them.

The Works of Viṣṇu—II

Page 47. This section speaks of the lord's accessibility (*saulabhya*)—beginning with Rāma's grace to everyone in his city Ayodhyā, ending with Kṛṣṇa as child. See pp. 4-13, for a section on Viṣṇu's prowess.

Page 48. For the myth of the Dwarf, see the note on 7.4.1 (p. 4). The poet here deftly fuses the figure of Bali with himself: the poem also plays on "knowing, incognito, unknowing, cheating." The god's mythic past patterns his dealings with the devotee, the speaker. The mythic past is the poet's present.

Page 49. Fish: Manu, the ancestor of all human beings, was washing his hands when a fish came into his hands asking to be saved and promising to save Manu from a flood. With his tending, the fish outgrew every vessel, bank, and river, till Manu carried it to the ocean (Viṣṇu the "expander"). In the year the fish had indicated, Manu built a ship, tied its rope to the horn of the giant fish, which took him through the waters to the northern mountain. The flood swept away all other creatures.

This is a very ancient myth, "even older than the Indo-European dispersal and the civilization of the Fertile Crescent, for the parallels with Semitic flood legends are striking." See O'Flaherty, *Hindu Myths*, pp. 179-84. The cowherd is Kṛṣṇa; for the Boar, see note to 7.4.3 (p. 6). The poem views the *avatāras* as special cases of Viṣṇu's myriad transformations.

Page 51. Note how in each stanza the Lord moves from the cosmic (Lakṣmī, three worlds, darker than the sea) to the homely (cowherd girl, banyan leaf, child on the speaker's hip). The cowherd girl is Piṉṉai, see p. 40 and note.

This is a rare poem in Nammāḻvār, who does not write often about the child Kṛṣṇa.

Love's Messengers

These "messenger" poems (called *tūtu*) follow a Sanskrit genre made famous by Kālidāsa in his *Cloud Messenger* (*Meghadūta*): in such poems, a lover sends a bird or other natural being with a message to his beloved. These simple-seeming poems have unexpected subtleties: in 1.4.7, p. 53, the wind threads through her bones, and the parrot is gnawing on a bone. The commentary notes that the parrot's beauty, its green body, red eyes and red mouth remind her of her lover Viṣṇu, who has those features. So the parrot too makes her ache for him, seems to be gnawing on her bones. Also, preoccupation with a bone makes the bird an indifferent messenger.

The commentators (see note 64 to Afterword) are allegory prone—they see the bird messengers as the teachers who bring the soul to god.

Idiots, Monists, and Others

Page 54. Being god-crazy is the badge of the true devotee. Afterword, pp. 117-121. The hill of cool waterfalls in Vēṅkaṭam.

Page 56. This piece gently savages monists, Śaṃkara's followers, who believe that the human soul and the divine are one, and that a realization of such a union is the true goal.

The monist believes, "I am Brahman." But a poem like 8.8.9 supports a belief in eternal individual souls that do not merge with god. The āḻvār wishes to serve, enjoy, and experience god forever, in the company of others like him, not to merge with god. As a popular saying goes, "One wants to taste the sugar, not become sugar." According to this poem, the true *māyā* of the monist is his belief in monism. See also p. 26.

Page 57. This mood of polemic is rare in Nammāḻvār—hence its inclusion. Other āḻvārs, like Tirumaḻicai and Tirumaṅkai, castigate the Śaivas, Buddhists, and Jainas.

No More Kings

Page 58. 3.9.7 plays on the conventional phrases of praise offered to kings in classical Tamil heroic poems. In bhakti, all the insignia of a king become the Lord's, as in South Indian temples—white umbrellas, elephants, yak tails, etc. In Tamil, *kō* means both "king" and "god"; *kōyil* means both "palace" and "temple." Notice also, throughout, that the master/man or lord/vassal relation is as important as the lover/beloved relation. As the chieftain or king divides and shares his plunder after war, the lord shares his infinite world. In Sanskrit, his name is *bhagavān* ("sharer of fortune"), derived from *bhaj*. This sharing of the spoils between the king and his henchmen is a bond of bhakti.

Love Poems: Four Returning Voices

Page 61. The six poems that follow are dramatic monologues spoken by four voices—a woman in love, her girlfriend, her foster mother, and the lover. The poetic mode, the personae, the moods, the details of landscape, etc., are all directly indebted to the classical Tamil conventions; with one difference—the lover is not a man but a god. See Afterword, pp. 157-160. The *Tiruviruttam* is a book of one hundred such love poems, which show Nammāḻvār's remarkable virtuosity in the use and renewal of classical poetic forms. In these poems, ancient voices return. *Viruttam* is a kind of meter; it also means an event, a story with characters, as here.

Page 63. The descriptions are formulaic as in classical Tamil love poems. Note how this love poem includes the *puṟam* warrior who cuts down demons, in an epithet.

Page 66. For a comparison with a classical parallel, see Afterword, p. 158.

My Lord, My Cannibal

Page 67. Afterword, p. 150.

Page 68. Kāṭkarai: a shrine

Love Poems: A Case of Possession

Page 70. The following six "mother's verses" (*tāypācuram*) fuse several themes: the beloved's crazy hallucinations of identity with her lover, the devotee's mystical oneness with his god, and possession, and the devotee as a mouthpiece of the god. In each poem, the girl in love identifies with a different aspect of Viṣṇu: incarnations, omnipresence, Viṣṇu as a source of all action, knowledge, and relations. Each poem rings changes on the god's epithets, the refrainlike repetitions (e.g., "world surrounded by the sea") and on the character of the listeners to whom the mother addresses her words. The words of the beloved, the mother's words, the description of the god and that of the listeners, all four chime and change with each other. See Afterword, p. 155.

The Takeover

Page 76. These poems from the very end of *Tiruvāymoḻi* climax the whole work. After these verses, we know what we didn't know fully before: all the verses so far were really the Lord's own making.

"The gardens" here and in the following refer to Tirumāliruñcōlai, as in 10.7.8, on p. 38.

Page 78. "City of names" is Tiruppērnakar. Pēr could mean either "name(s)" or "great." Pērnakar could also be "great city."

Page 83. The cosmic Lord of the incarnations who came down to save the worlds here comes down and "becomes" the servant. For allusions, see notes to 7.4.1-3, 7.4.6, on pp. 4-6, 9. Kalki is the future incarnation of Viṣṇu, who will appear at the end of the present age. He will take the form of an invading horseman on a white stallion, destroy all foreign invaders and heretics such as the Buddhists, overturn the wicked Kali Age (the present), and bring on a new cycle of time. One *avatāra* of the traditional ten, the Buddha, is never mentioned by the āḻvār. (The *avatāra* is an ambiguous one, for Viṣṇu becomes the Buddha in this myth only to delude and ruin the demons with an evil doctrine. See O'Flaherty, *Hindu Myths*, p. 231.)

The poem includes the past incarnations and the future one of Kalki, and ends with the lord in the present, the lord dark as raincloud who is all of them, and the speaker too.

Afterword

In this Afterword on early Tamil Bhakti, I attempt a mosaic of ideas, some well known, some less so. Nammāḻvār composes unique poems out of shared materials, a great common stock of ideas, forms, and motifs. Poetry such as Nammāḻvār's, at the head of a living tradition, has formed Indian conceptions of bhakti and given bhakti its figures and meanings. Such works are texts as well as contexts.

The Great Shift

A great, many-sided shift[1] occurred in Hindu culture and sensibility between the sixth and ninth century—or so it seems to that hindsight we sometimes call a sense of history. Bhakti[2] is one name for that shift.

[1] The phrase "shift in Hindu culture and sensibility" will gain precision as we move through my argument. At this stage, it is vague and needs defense. I use the word "shift" to suggest a linguistic analogy, for example, the "great consonantal shift," precisely described in Indo-European linguistics. The linguistic model of change implies that the shift is systematic, begins in a small way, in a particular locality or even community, and slowly spreads from there in waves, depending on a variety of conditions; the innovation does *not* universally *replace* the older forms, but develops a parallel existence that may come to dominate, cross, and transform the relevant, older linguistic or cultural forms—in this case, religious conceptions, practices, and patterns of feeling expressed by them. It is this complex of concepts, practices, patterns of feeling coupled with their artistic expression in texts, temples, etc., that I call "sensibility" here.

[2] A dictionary entry (adapted from M. Monier-Williams, *Sanskrit-English Dictionary*, Oxford, 1956, p. 743) might be useful, however treacherous. *Bhakti* is derived from the root *bhaj*:

Early bhakti movements, whether devoted to Śiva or to Viṣṇu, used whatever they found at hand, and changed whatever they used. Vedic and Upaniṣadic notions, Buddhist and Jaina concepts, conventions of Tamil and Sanskrit poetry, early Tamil conceptions of love, service, women, and kings, mythology or folk religion and folksong, the play of contrasts between Sanskrit and the mother tongue: all these elements were reworked and transformed in bhakti.

Developments in the north, during the period of the Guptas (A.D. 320-540) truly prepared the ground.[3] For instance, the Gupta kings called themselves devotees of god (*bhāgavatas*). They took the names of the gods, put the figures of Lakṣmī, Viṣṇu's consort, and Varāha, his incarnation as a boar, on their coins, and made mythology a state concern, enlisting particularly Viṣṇu and his heroic incarnations for their politics. The Guptas sponsored Viṣṇu and almost believed that Viṣṇu

---

bhaj to divide, distribute, allot or apportion to, share with; to grant, bestow, furnish, supply;
to obtain as one's share, receive as, partake of, enjoy (also carnally), possess, have;
to turn or resort to, engage in, assume (as a form), put on (garments), experience, incur, undergo, feel, go or fall into (with acc., esp. of abstract noun; e.g., *bhītim*, to feel terror);
to pursue, practise, cultivate;
to declare for, to prefer, choose (e.g., as a servant);
to serve, honour, revere, love, adore. . . .

In these pages, I use "bhakti" as a short-hand term for a whole complex of sects, beliefs, texts, and so forth. Nammāḻvār's is only one kind of bhakti. For another kind, the bhakti of the Vīraśaivas, see A. K. Ramanujan, *Speaking of Śiva*.

[3] The Guptas: Radha Kumud Mookerji, *The Gupta Empire*; Romila Thapar, *A History of India*, chap. 7.

sponsored the Gupta Empire. Kṛṣṇa as a god with his own legends and cults emerged in the later Gupta period. Not only were the first Hindu temples built and the first Hindu icons sculptured during this period, but the official forms of Hindu mythology were set down in great syncretic texts called purāṇas. By the fifth century, Viṣṇu, Śiva, their families, minions, and enemies seem to have become as real as the human dynasties.

The Guptas were also great patrons of Sanskrit. Sanskrit, "classical Sanskrit," was the language not only of the gods; it became the language of royal inscriptions, court poetry, theater, and the sciences. Of the oral and vernacular traditions, whatever was deemed worthy of preserving (be it medical, astrological, or astronomical lore, or one of the many cycles of legends and tales) soon acquired a second, parallel life, often an authorized version, in Sanskrit texts. Sanskrit preserved, as in amber, much that was oral in the local, "little" traditions, and in this special and precise sense, Sanskrit *sanskritized*.

In South India, by the sixth century, the Pallavas ("sprouts"?) had arrived. Their inscriptions record the end of one era in South Indian history and the beginning of a new one. In the culture of this time, the two "classicisms" of India, that of the Guptas and that of Tamil classical poetry, seem to have met.

For three hundred years (6th-9th century), two dynasties, the Pallavas of Kāñcī and the Pāṇṭiyas of Madurai (farther south), dominated the Tamil region and waged wars with each other and with the neighboring Deccan kingdoms. Yet in the midst of raging battles and shifting boundaries, cultural expression blossomed, especially in Pallava country. One is forcefully reminded of Shakespeare's question (Sonnet 65):

How with this rage shall beauty hold a plea,
Whose action is no stronger than a flower?

Not only did poetry, sainthood, and art "hold a plea," they helped renew, unify, and reconstruct the culture.

Sanskrit, brahmans, and temples were part of the imperial design. The Sanskrit language gave dignity and resonance to an upstart king; brahmans blessed and legitimized him, often gave him a genealogy if he lacked one; and temples assured town and village of his presence, his patronage, and his fidelity to a popular god. All three enlisted the gods.

The creative Pallava artist-king Mahendravarman I (A.D. 604-630) covered himself with resonant titles in his inscriptions. In one he called himself *vicitracitta*, "versatile in mind," and he deserved the title: he painted, composed music, and patronized Sanskrit, even wrote a farce in it. In an inscription, he announced his joy in his first rock-cut temples: "not the soft sandstone, but from obdurate granite . . . this brickless, timberless, metalless, mortarless mansion."[4]

He and his successors gave village lands to temples and brahmans joining in new ways brahman to peasant, royal center to rural periphery—and Sanskrit to Tamil.[5] Tank irrigation converted dry or forested land

[4] At Mandagapaṭṭu (South Arcot district). See T. V. Mahalingam, *Kāñcīpuram in Early South Indian History*, p. 71. The translation is Kathi Rose's.

[5] The languages they chose for their inscriptions reflect changes in audience. Pallava inscriptions were first in Prakrit, then in Sanskrit, finally in Sanskrit and Tamil. The language choices record the rise of a local dynasty to "imperial" status, to "the first Tamil dynasty of real consequence" (Thapar, p. 169). See Thapar, p. 178, for an A.D. 783 copper grant document, which begins in Sanskrit with a eulogy to the king and continues in Tamil to record the details of the grant (the land, the use of the water, the houses, etc.).

to prosperous agriculture. Meanwhile, saints' pilgrimages and celebratory songs about hundreds of holy places mapped the country much as the king's institutions did; they literally sang places into existence.[6] Music, sculpture, painting, and philosophy were part of

[6] Although the saints lived in Pāṇṭiya and Cēra kingdoms also, I speak here, and summarily, only of the early Pallavas because they seem to set the patterns.

The Śaiva saints celebrate 274 holy places; the Vaiṣṇavas, 108, of which 106 are terrestrial and 2 celestial, that is, Viṣṇu's paradise Vaikuntam, and the Ocean of Milk where he sleeps. Nammāḻvār wrote poems about 30 places. The 108 places were called *divyadeśam* "divine places," *pāṭalpeṟṟa patikaḷ* "places that received a song." See Katherine Young, "Beloved Places (Ukantaruḷiṉanilaṅkaḷ)," on the subject. See also "Religious and Cultural Sites, 8th-12th Centuries," Plate IV.4, in Joseph B. Schwartzberg, *A Historical Atlas of South Asia*, p. 34: the map plots the birthplaces and dates of Vaiṣṇava and Śaiva saints and philosophers in South India.

Names of places, waters, peaks, headlands, etc., like persons, objects, and acts associated with the lord, were renamed with the suffix *tiru-* "holy, auspicious."

The temples were just as "utilitarian" as dams and canals. "Public works like the latter were often administered under the auspices of temples from the middle Pallava period through at least the Vijayanagar period." Nicholas B. Dirks, "Political Authority and Structural Change in Early South Indian History," pp. 145-46. For new thinking about South Indian temples, see Burton Stein, ed., "Special Number on South Indian Temples." Although the essays are about a later period, they are relevant. Temples are "the most sensitive institution registering changes . . . especially of dominance patterns"; they are witnesses to the South Indian conception that "human leaders (kings both large and small . . .), and the deities installed in temples, *share* sovereignty." South Indian "political communities are *communities of worship*. . . . The temple is the cultural and ideological context in which men and resources can be controlled, authority contested, and kingship revitalized" (Stein, p. 7). See also Arjun Appadurai in the same issue for a discussion of "the dynamic pan-regional network . . . and the temples as redistributive centers, where gifts to deities enabled the continuous transformation of material sources into status and authority" (p.

this creative upsurge—and "these overflowed into the numerous Hindu colonies across the sea."[7]

At such a time of war, change, and reordering, Nammālvār's poem of creation seems especially expressive and apt:

First, the discus
  rose to view,

then the conch,
    the long bow,
    the mace,
    and the sword;

with blessings
  from the eight quarters,

he broke through
  the egg-shell of heaven,
    making the waters bubble;

giant head and giant feet
  growing away from each other,

time itself rose to view:

how the lord
  paced and measured

all three worlds!

7.4.1

It speaks of the warrior-god Viṣṇu, his insignia (discus, conch, bow, mace, sword), the hatching of the

73). For a fuller historical treatment of a Vaiṣṇava temple, see Arjun Appadurai, "Worship and Conflict in South India: The Case of the Śrī Pārtasārati Svāmi Temple 1800-1973." See also K. Gnanambal, "Srivaishnavas and Their Religious Institutions," and V. N. Hari Rao, *Kōil Olugu, the Chronicle of the Srīrangam Temple, with Historical Notes*, for temple records.

[7] K. A. Nilakanta Sastri, *A History of South India*, p. 147.

world, a giant body growing out of his dwarfish Vāmana form, and his act of measuring the worlds with his strides. Viṣṇu means "pervader, expander." The word *ūḻi* that I have translated as "time" could have been translated as "a (new) age," or "an earth."

The saints were not flunkies; they often defied the kings and the times. Yet, in their religious idiom, they showed "the form and pressure" of the age.

The First Bhakti Poems

The imperial presence of Sanskrit, with its brahmanical (*smṛti*) texts of the Vedas and the Upaniṣads, was a presence against which bhakti in Tamil defines itself, though not always defiantly. Bhakti, it has been suggested, arises out of the meeting of Sanskritic religion and mythology with Tamil conceptions of women and kings.[8]

Two late classical Tamil anthologies contain the earliest bhakti poems. The *Paripāṭal* (6th century?) has seven hymns to Tirumāl (Viṣṇu/Kṛṣṇa) and eight to Murukaṉ. The gods are given the full panoply of San-

[8] George L. Hart III, "The Nature of Tamil Devotion," p. 113, summarizes the position well:

> [In indigenous South Indian religion] power was not something summoned from another world, such as the gods in the Ṛgveda; it was immanent in the things one comes into contact with every day. . . . When the North Indian gods were imported and had to find a place in South India, . . . the new god was modeled on and assimilated to the king; . . . many Tamil terms for the North Indian god first meant king or still can mean either king or god; the temple is constructed like a palace; and the deity is treated like a king, being awakened in the morning by auspicious music, getting married, and receiving many of the same ceremonies as the human king.

skritic myths, epithets, and motifs. The poems blend the erotic, the heroic, and the sacred, as later bhakti poems do.

For the first time in India, Hindu philosophy and theology speak in a language other than Sanskrit:

> In fire, you are the heat; in blossoms, the
> fragrance;
> among the stones, you are the diamond;
> in speech, truth;
> among virtues, you are love; in valor—strength;
> in the Veda, you are the secret; among
> elements, the primordial;
> in the burning sun, the light; in moonlight,
> its sweetness;
> You are all, and you are the substance
> and meaning of all.[9]

Furthermore, the text speaks of itself as a blend of music (*icai*) and poetry (*iyal*), probably accompanied by mime (*avinayam*). With these features of content, form, and performance, the fifteen *Paripāṭal* poems about Viṣṇu and Murukaṉ may be considered the first bhakti hymns.

The other late-classical poem, *Tirumurukāṟṟuppaṭai*, "A Guide to Lord Murukaṉ" is the earliest, long, full-fledged bhakti poem. Composed in about the sixth century, it grafts the oldest Tamil conceptions of heroes to Sanskritic ideas and mythologies. Murukaṉ is the Tamil god of beauty, youth, love and war. Like Viṣṇu, he is willing to battle with enemies whenever they appear.

A legend goes with the poem. A demon captured the poet Nakkīrar and kept him in a cave where he had

[9] *Paripāṭal* III.63-68, translated by Kamil Zvelebil, "The Beginnings of Bhakti in South India," p. 255.

already trapped 999 men for a sacrifice. Lord Murukaṉ appeared, killed the demon, and saved the poet and all the others. The poem was written in the cave; was said to have the power to save anyone who recites it.

In the face of terror
his faces, faces of comfort, appear;
in the battlefield, his lance
  says, "Do not fear!"
Think of him once in your heart:
he will appear twice
to anyone who says, "Murukā!"[10]

This poem bridges the classical period and the period of bhakti. The poem was not only included in the latest classical anthology *Pattuppāṭṭu* ("Ten Songs"); it became an important part of the eleventh *Tirumuṟai*, the Śaiva canon.[11]

In form, the poem is a classical guide poem (*āṟṟuppaṭai*),[12] in which one poet directs another to a generous heroic patron and his place through descrip-

[10] My translation of a quatrain quoted by Kamil Zvelebil, *Tamil Literature*, p. 103n.

[11] Ibid., pp. 103-104.

[12] Here, and later, I assume an acquaintance with classical Tamil poetry, though my examples are intended to be self-explanatory. For translations and discussions of classical Tamil poetry, see A. K. Ramanujan, *The Interior Landscape, Love Poems from a Classical Tamil Anthology*; Kamil Zvelebil, *A History of Tamil Literature*; George L. Hart III, *The Poems of Ancient Tamil: Their Milieu and Their Sanskrit Counterparts*, and *The Poets of the Tamil Anthologies*. See Hart, *Poems* and *Poets*, and Kailasapathy, *Tamil Heroic Poetry*, for examples of *puṟam* poems and the character of the chieftains, their generosity and their prowess in virtuous battle—both these characteristics are attributes of Viṣṇu in mythology and in the āḻvār's poems. The importance of the goddess Lakṣmī, his consort, also parallels the importance of the *puṟam* chieftain's chaste spouse. If we assume (as we should, I think) that the *akam* love poems are about the same

tions of how to get there and what he will find there. It is also a praise poem in the heroic (*puṟam*) tradition.

In *A Guide to Lord Murukaṉ*, the guide poem and the heroic praise poem have become devotional; the subject is a god instead of a human hero. The motifs, the landscapes, the moods of awe, love, and supplication, are directly in the classical Tamil heroic (*puṟam*) tradition. Murukaṉ is both lover and chieftain; the interior (*akam*) and the exterior (*puṟam*), love and war, meet in him.

The poem has six parts, each devoted to a temple or place of Murukaṉ to which the pilgrim is guided. The six holy places, the six parts of this poem, and the six faces of Murukaṉ are homologues of each other—so the topography is rendered mystic and sacred. Sanskritic myths and motifs are subordinated to an early Tamil genre. Viṣṇu, Śiva, Indra, and Brahma, the four great Hindu gods, are subordinated to Murukaṉ. The double espousal of Murukaṉ is also significant: he has two wives, a heavenly Sanskritic Teyvayāṉai, and an earthly Vaḷḷi of Tamil folklore.

I shall quote only one relevant section of this first great bhakti poem to make my next point:

> The possessed shaman with the spear
> wears wreaths of green leaves
>   with aromatic nuts between them
> and beautiful long pepper,

---

chieftains in a different setting, the parallels with Kṛṣṇa's loves are striking.

Akam and *puṟam*, the poetry of love and war, are both important precedents for bhakti. Not much attention has so far been paid to the *puṟam* precedents. It is significant that the first long bhakti poem is an *āṟṟuppaṭai*, a "guide poem." Just as the classical Tamil bard wandered, visited, and praised patrons, the saints, too, wandered to the holy places and sang of them and the gods there.

wild jasmine and the three-lobed
white nightshade;

his jungle tribes
have chests bright with sandal;
the strong-bowed warriors
in their mountain village
drink with their kin
sweet liquor, honey brew
aged in long bamboos,
they dance rough dances
hand in hand
to the beat of small
hillside drums;

the women
wear wreaths of buds
fingered and forced to blossom
so they smell differently,
wear garlands
from the pools on the hill
all woven into chains,

cannabis leaves
in their dense hair,

white clusters
from a sacred *kaṭampu* tree
red-trunked and flowering,
arrayed between large cool leaves
for the male beetle to suck at,

in leaf-skirts
shaking
on their jeweled mounds of venus,
and their gait sways with the innocence
of peacocks;

the shaman
is the Red One himself,
is in red robes;

young leaf of the red-trunk *aśoka*
flutter in his ears;

He wears a coat of mail,
  a warrior band on his ankle,
    a wreath of scarlet ixora;

has a flute,
  a horn,
  several small instruments
  of music;

for vehicles
  he has a ram,
  a peacock;

a faultless rooster
  on his banner;

the Tall One
  with bracelets on his arms,
  with a bevy of girls, voices
    like lutestrings,
a cloth
cool-looking above the waist-band
tied so it hangs
all the way to the ground;

his hands large
  as drumheads
  hold gently
  several soft-shouldered
    fawnlike women;

he gives them proper places

and he dances
on the hills:

and all such things happen
because
of His being
there.

And not only there.

"A Guide to Lord Murukaṉ"
(*Tirumurukāṟṟuppaṭai*)

Murukaṉ and his motifs appear in the earliest Tamil poems. He is a god of the mountain (*kuṟiñci*), one of the five landscapes of classical poetry; he is the Red One, god of love, war, and fertility. The poem pictures a whole community of men and women, with a god amid them, drinking, dancing, singing; the flowers and leaves they wear are emblematic of both erotic and warlike moods. When the poem ends, the chief dancer and the god he worships have become one. The dancer does not simply worship or adore the god; he invokes the god by representing him. He dances the god's dance, he wears the Red One's robes and insignia, carries His lance (*vēl*), imitating the god till he becomes Him, simulating Him until he is assimilated. The words *murukaṉ* and *vēlaṉ* (the one with the lance) mean both the god and the shamanic priest who is his devotee.

The poem evokes the primal, the essential experience of bhakti: not ecstasy, not enstasy,[13] but an embodi-

[13] For the various relations between shamanism and yoga, see Mircea Eliade, *Yoga, Immortality, and Freedom*; for an anthropological account of spirit possession, I. M. Lewis, *Ecstatic Religion, An Anthropological Study of Spirit Possession and Shamanism*. The parallels between shamanism and bhakti cults (e.g., marriage to a god) are

ment; neither a shamanic flight to the heavens or soul loss, nor a yogic autonomy, a withdrawal of the senses—but a partaking of the god. He may pass through enstasy (withdrawal) and ecstasy (out-of-body experiences) as stages. Like certain shamans, a bhakta seeks to be a place, a vessel, for his chosen spirit who has chosen him.

My head
  is the hill
    of the lord's gardens
  the ocean of milk

my body
  the paradisal dwelling-place of Viṣṇu
  Vēṅkaṭam hill
    cool and holy . . .

Nammāḻvār 10.7.8

A bhakta is not content to worship a god in word and ritual, nor is he content to grasp him in a theology; he needs to possess him and be possessed by him. He needs also to sing, to dance; to make poetry, painting, shrines, sculpture; to embody him in every possible way. In bhakti, all the arts become also "techniques of ecstasy," incitements to possession.

Arthur Nock has said, "The primitive does not worship, he dances his god."[14] We could bracket "primi-

worth pursuing. For ecstasy, enstasy, see Eliade, *Yoga*, p. 339. Lewis, p. 51, disagrees with Eliade—the shaman's body, like the āḻvār's, is a "placing," a receptacle for spirits (see next section). Compare also the Murukaṉ passage above with Shirokogoff's description of a Tungus shaman: "The rhythmic music and singing, and later the dancing of the shaman, gradually involve every participant more and more in a collective action. . . . In shamanizing, the audience at the same time acts and participates." Lewis, p. 53.

[14] I quote from memory and cannot trace the Nock quotation.

tive" in quotation marks and interpret the word as primal, original, aboriginal in experience, not necessarily in time. One of the earliest cave paintings of early man is that of a dancing sorcerer: he appears not only in the upper paleolithic caves of 16,000 B.C., and in the mythologies of American Indians and elsewhere,[15] but in the myths and arts of the Hindus, especially in the cults and dancing forms of Kṛṣṇa, Śiva, Ganeśa, and the goddess (Śakti). The Tamil word for shaman is *cāmiyāṭi*, "god-dancer." Some aspect of a god dancing, and man "dancing his god," is present in all bhakti.

"Possession" and Bhakti[16]

Veṟi, or "frenzy," is a mood often described in Tamil war poems and in bhakti poems. The devotee is often called demon, madman, idiot (*pēy*, *pittaṉ*).

Nammāḻvār speaks frequently of being entered, filled, taken over, enslaved as well as enabled by a divine being:

Promising me heaven,
  making a pact with me,

today he entered this nest,
  this thing of flesh,

himself cleared away
  all obstacles
    to himself,
  all contrary acts,

[15] Weston LaBarre, *The Ghost Dance: Origins of Religion.*

[16] For earlier discussions, see Louis Dumont, "Renunciation in World Religions," and Glenn E. Yocum, "Shrines, Shamanism, and Love Poetry: Elements in the Emergence of Popular Tamil Bhakti."

our lord of the good city
        of names,
whose groves are humming with bees.

Nammāḻvār 10.8.5

Māṇikkavācakar (9th century Śaiva saint) describes the violence of such a possession:

He grabbed me
  lest I go astray.

Wax before an unspent fire,
  mind melted,
  body trembled.

I bowed, I wept,
  danced, cried aloud,
  I sang, and I praised him.

Unyielding, as they say,
  as an elephant's jaw
  or a woman's grasp,
  was love's unrelenting
  seizure.

Love pierced me
  like a nail
    driven into a green tree.

Overflowing, I tossed
  like a sea,

heart growing tender,
body shivering,

while the world called me Demon!
and laughed at me,

I left shame behind,

took as an ornament
  the mockery of the local folk.
Unswerving, I lost my cleverness
  in the bewilderment of ecstasy.

Tiruvācakam: IV.59-70[17]

In the classical poem on Murukan̲ (pp. 112-115), the god and the possession are described, framed, as "objects" seen from an onlooker's point of view; it is happening *out there* to a shaman. In the two bhakti poems it happens to the speaker, the subject.[18] This is an important qualitative shift. Furthermore, such frenzy is seen as the mark of the bhakta. In the following poem, "craziness" has become *de rigueur*, almost a prescription, a necessary credential. Bypassing city and civilization, the devotee courts ridicule.

Mumbling and prattling
  the many names
    of our lord of the hill
with cool waterfalls,
  long strands of water,

while onlookers say,
  "They're crazy,"

entering and not entering
  cities,

[17] I am indebted to Yocum, "Shrines," for this reference. For Tiruvācakam translations, see G. U. Pope, *Tiruvācagam or "Sacred Utterances" of the Tamil Poet, Saint, and Sage Māṇikka-vācagar*, and Glenn E. Yocum, "A Study of Māṇikkavācakar's Tiruvācakam: The Setting and Significance of a Tamil Devotional Text."

[18] For earlier discussion of this shift of attention from the "object" to the "subject," see Zvelebil's summary of A. M. Pyatigorsky's Russian work, *Materiali po istorii indijskoj filosofii* (Moscow, 1962) in Kamil Zvelebil, *The Smile of Murugan*, pp. 199-200. Also Ramanujan, *Speaking of Śiva*, pp. 40-41.

standing still or swaying
  before a laughing world,

they dance, they leap,
  undone by feeling—

and the gods bow down
  before them.

Nammāḻvār 3.5.8[19]

The poets make poetry out of such a possession; their god is their "genius."

Poets,
  beware, your life is in danger:

the lord of gardens is a thief,
  a cheat,
master of illusions;
he came to me,
  a wizard with words,
  sneaked into my body,
    my breath,

with bystanders looking on
  but seeing nothing,
he consumed me
  life and limb,

and filled me,
  made me over
into himself.

Nammāḻvār 10.7.1

Such an association of poetry and possession is not new. The Vedas spoke of "quivering seers (*vipras*),"[20] shakers and quakers, and poets (*kavis*) who were of that

[19] From now on, unless otherwise noted, numbers given without further reference indicate poems from Nammāḻvār's *Tiruvāymoḻi*.

[20] J. F. Staal, "Sanskrit and Sanskritization," p. 267. The root *vip-*

visionary company. If originality is often a return to the origins, bhakti is such a return, a creative regression. The Vedas are not textual precedents for bhakti, for most of the saints had no access to them: of the twelve āḻvārs, only two were brahmans, one was an untouchable, one a woman. But like the Vedas they speak the language of possession, for they experience in themselves what Vedic seers experienced when they "saw." They "climb to their proper dark" as the earlier poet-seers did, as all such seers must.

From Possession to Incarnation: An Āḻvār Poem Analyzed

From possession to incarnation is a small step—in both, the god descends. *Avatāra*, the Sanskrit word for incarnation, means "descent."[21] It is especially a small step if one thinks that the creator is all of creation; then, all created things are incarnations.

The famous *avatāras* of Viṣṇu as fish, cowherd, wild boar, and so forth were only spectacular cases of the Lord's myriad labors:

Before I could say,
"He became cowherd

in *vipra* denotes "trembling, quivering," etymologically related to the English word "vibration." The root *vip-* is also used to describe the mystical intoxication of the Vedic poets, who have been inspired by the gods. But later, a *vipra* is (only) a brahman by birth, sacraments, and knowledge.

[21] The āḻvārs, like the authors of the earlier purāṇas, seem to have no notion of a limited number of *avatāras*. See Friedhelm Hardy, "Ideology and Cultural Contexts of the Śrīvaiṣṇava Temple"; and Cornelia Dimmitt and J.A.B. van Buitenen, eds. and trans., *Classical Hindu Mythology, a Reader in the Sanskrit Purāṇas.*

fish
wild boar,"
he became a million million.

1.8.8

Nammāḻvār's 1.1.4 is an apt text for this theme:

nām avaṉ ivaṉ uvaṉ
avaḷ ivaḷ uvaḷ evaḷ
tām avar ivar uvar
atu itu utu etu
vīm avai ivai uvai
avai nalam tīṅku avai
ām avai āy avai
āy niṉṟa avarē

We here and that man, this man,
and that other in-between,
and that woman, this woman,
and that other, whoever,

those people, and these,
and these others in-between,
this thing, that thing,
and this other in-between, whichever,

all things dying, these things,
those things, those others in-between,
good things, bad things,
things that were, that will be,

being all of them,
he stands there.

Let us look at this poem closely:
1. The first half of the poem looks like a grammatical paradigm, a breathless recital of Tamil pronouns. Old Tamil has three kinds of "pointing" in pronouns, with

an affix for each: *a-* denotes "that one (he, she, or it) there" (e.g., *avaṉ*); *i-* denotes "this one here" (e.g., *ivaṉ*); *u-* denotes "the one that is in-between" (e.g., *uvaṉ*). The three kinds of pronouns,—"this," "that," and "the other in-between"—divide the universe among them. As words, such pronouns are rather special: although most general in their reference, they point to real particulars in the living context outside the language. A pronoun like "he" refers to a generalized male person, yet points to an actual particular person *out there* in the world where the speech-event occurs. Such words are called "shifters";[22] they mediate between speech and speaking, between language and the context in which language lives. Thus the poem, in using such shifters, is both most general in naming all possible people and objects and most particular in pointing to the very people and objects in the audience at the moment of speaking.

2. Observe how the poem is enclosed between "We here" (*nām*) and "he there," the Lord (*avarē*); contained between these two are all things, all persons, all beings.

3. After the long enumeration of the many, the many is folded back into the one—the poem's movement enacts this becoming of the many into the one. The subject of the sentence comes at the end, with the last word, *avar*, "he," the Lord: the subject-predicate order in the sentence is actually inverted. The *sentence* speaks of the one proliferating into the many; but in the way it begins and ends, the *poem* moves from the many to the one—as if the two opposite aspects are the same. The enfolding and the unfolding are the same thing

[22] "Shifters" or "indexes" (in C. S. Peirce's semiotics) are types of signs whose meaning always involves some object of the context in which the sign occurs. Pronouns are good examples of shifters. Roman Jakobson, *Shifters, Verbal Categories, and the Russian Verb.*

seen from different directions. The Lord is one, becomes many, yet remains one. Everything is thus an incarnation; and it is a process, it is continuous. So the word *āku* "become" is used many times, in several tenses: *āy* "having become," *ākum* "(the one) who becomes, who will become," *āy niṉṟa* "(who) has become," and so forth.

4. Within all this teeming process is a central stasis—just as, after all the tenses of past and future, the poem ends with a participle qualifying "him," in *āy niṉṟa avarē*, "he who stands there, or is there, having become (all things and persons)." *Nīṉṟa-tu* means "that which is permanent; immovable; remainder, as standing over."

5. Though he has become, and is, all of the things mentioned, he is not them—he "stands there," apart. The Vaiṣṇavas have a pair of technical terms, *paratvam* "otherness," and *saulabhyam* "ease of access."[23] He is everything, yet the other. He is at hand, easy of access; yet beyond. The Murukaṉ poem quoted earlier crystallizes this central paradox and twofold attribute. At the end of every one of its six sections, we have a line that says, "He is here, but not only here." He is local,

[23] For a fuller discussion of *paratvam* and *saulabhyam*, see John B. Carman, *The Theology of Rāmānuja, an Essay in Interreligious Understanding*, pp. 244-48 and elsewhere. Carman, p. 249 cites a charming analogy attributed to Rāmānuja. "How can a lame man climb on an elephant if you tell him to do so? Likewise how can an insignificant soul in this imperfect world approach the lord of all? The answer is surely that an elephant can accommodate itself, lying down so that the lame man can mount." Carman translates *paratvam* as "supremacy." These two terms, *paratvam* and *saulabhyam*, look like, but should be distinguished from, transcendence and immanence. The latter pair speaks of God's objective ontological characteristics; the Vaiṣṇava pair speaks of the Lord as seen from the devotee's point of view. The Vaiṣṇava is a "phenomenologist."

yet translocal; located yet unconfined—an important motif in early bhakti.

6. The verb *āku* in Tamil can mean both "be" and "become." *Āy niṉṟa* as an attribute of Viṣṇu has both the following meanings: "being," "having become." *Āy* has also the sense of "acting as, in the role of." The Lord's playacting and make-believe (*līlā* "sport") are part of the suggestion.

7. The pronouns (*avaṉ/ivaṉ*, *avaḷ/ivaḷ*, etc.) with their changing affixes are a set of related words with family resemblances. This use of "paradigmatic" sets, sets of changing but similar-sounding forms, is a common poetic technique in these poems. In addition, the poems are arranged in groups of ten, and each group shares a set of themes and a family of word forms.

8. We may note also the way the *Tiruvāymoḻi* poems of Nammāḻvār are linked to each other. Each poem begins with the last word of the previous poem,[24] all the way to the last poem whose last word returns to the first word of the first poem, across 1,000 and more poems. This linking device is called *antāti* (Sanskrit *anta* "end," *ādi* "beginning"). But the repeated words, though they look alike, may mean new things. *Avar* as it ends 1.1.4 does not mean the same as the *avar* that opens 1.1.5. In 1.1.4, it means, "he (the lord)"; in 1.1.5, *avaravar* means "each person."

In this kind of play on words, in the use of sets of related words, the same physical forms are constantly transformed; the same words are given new meanings in an intricate play. These formal patterns are paralleled by the theme of the Lord's myriad forms and transfor-

[24] With minor exceptions: 1.6.1 ends with *pū(vē)*, 1.6.2 begins with *matu*. Probably the connection is semantic, as G. Damodaran, *Ācārya Hṛdayam*, pp. 230-31, suggests: *pū* "flower," *matu* "honey."

mations. We get an impression, a sensation almost, of the many forms of the one.

Thus, in a poem like 1.1.4, grammar becomes poetry, and poetry becomes theology. If one may be fanciful, the "present perfect" here describes both a grammatical form and the form of the divine. Conceptions of god are enacted by word and syntax; furthermore, god's one-and-manyness becomes the living word to be uttered, danced to, sung and chanted in temples as these poems are to this day.

The Language of Bhakti: Sanskrit and the Mother Tongue

It is not surprising that the first bhakti poets appeared in the Tamil-speaking areas. Tamil was the one Indian *mother tongue* with a long literary tradition going back to at least the first century A.D. or B.C. We must remember that the only literary languages by the time of the Guptas were Sanskrit and its Prakrit relatives.[25]

[25] The relation of Vedic Sanskrit, classical Sanskrit, the various Prakrits, and the concurrent regional dialects is complex. See George Cardona, "Indo-Aryan Languages," for a succinct statement. The most archaic literary Prakrit is Pāli, the language of the Buddhist canon (ca. 5th century B.C.). Ardhamāgadhī was the chief language of the early Jaina canon. Buddhists also wrote in a Buddhist Hybrid Sanskrit. The Apabhraṃśa ("corrupt") dialect of Middle Indo-Aryan was used as a literary language by the 6th century A.D. All these forms are standardizations of regional varieties. Thus, even within the Sanskrit-Prakrit-dialect complex, even in the diction of any one variety, there were degrees of "Sanskritization," of which Classical Sanskrit was the supreme example.

The Buddhists and the Jainas were the first de-Sanskritizers: Buddha enjoined his followers to use the vernaculars. Aśoka used Middle Indo-Aryan, not Sanskrit, in the inscriptions of his kingdom. As we shall see, these are not the only parallels between Buddhism and Jainism, and the Hindu bhakti sects.

None of them was spoken as a workaday language. Even Kālidāsa, the greatest poet of classical Sanskrit (5th century A.D.), must have been bilingual: using Sanskrit for court and composition, and a spoken dialect of Ujjain(?) for family and daily affairs. The spoken regional dialects that later became the modern Indo-Aryan languages such as Bengali, Gujerati, Marathi, and varieties of Hindi, did not have any literary form until after the tenth century.

The dialogue, the dialectic, between Sanskrit and Tamil was not simple. Even in the Tamil-speaking region (spanning today's Tamilnadu and Kerala), some poetry and all Hindu philosophy was composed in Sanskrit. To our knowledge, the great southern philosopher Rāmānuja (11th-12th century) never wrote a word in Tamil or cited a Tamil text.[26] Sanskrit had antiquity, hieratic pan-Indian prestige; it was the lingua franca of pundits, philosophers, epic poets, lawgivers, courts, and kings. It was unrivaled as model, metalanguage, as a source of forms, a standard, an ancestor even to languages unrelated to it. Sanskrit was culture.

As noted in the Introduction, a Vedic model was never far from the minds of the brahman compilers of the Tamil hymns.[27] The Four Thousand were called the Tamil Vedas, the Drāviḍa Upaniṣads. The āḻvārs themselves often spoke of Sanskrit and Tamil in the same

[26] On a number of points, Rāmānuja's disciples were closer to the Tamil tradition than their master, e.g., on the importance of Goddess Lakṣmī as a mediatrix (*puruṣakāra*). See Carman, p. 244.

[27] See van Buitenen, pp. 30-36, on the Vedic model, and the ācāryas' need to "Sanskritize," to restate the Tamil tradition in relation to a sacral past. "Central to Indian thinking through the ages is a concept of knowledge which, though known to Platonism and Gnosticism, is foreign to the modern West. Whereas for us, to put it briefly, knowledge is something to be *discovered*, for the Indian knowledge is to be *recovered*." Van Buitenen, p. 35.

breath, though they were careful to distinguish their own poems from the Vedas (see below). The Vaiṣṇava theologians called their philosophy *ubhayavedānta*, "the two-fold philosophy," facing both ways, reconciling Sanskritic and Tamil thought. To express this blend, commentators on the Tamil poems developed an enlarged alphabet and a highly Sanskritized Tamil called *maṇipravāḷa*. *Maṇipravāḷa* meant a stringing together of Sanskrit diamond, *maṇi*, and Tamil coral, *pravāḷa*.[28]

Yet Tamil was dear to the poets and theologians.[29] Tamil alone had a full-grown literary courtly tradition as well as oral and village folk traditions—which "qualified" Tamil as a real alternative, in the culture of the time, for popular religious compositions.

Similar linguistic and political reasons seem to "qualify" Kannada as the next language for bhakti expression: Pampa's great court epics were composed in the

[28] On *maṇipravāḷa* literature, see K.K.A. Venkatachari, *The Maṇipravāla Literature of the Śrīvaiṣṇava Ācāryas, 12th to 15th Century A.D.*

[29] From the 13th century on, the commentators debate endlessly the relative virtues of Sanskrit and Tamil as religious languages. For a list of pros and cons, see Venkatachari, pp. 25-27. One story about the tension in this dual heritage is poignant: Vaṅkīpurattu Nampi, a disciple of Rāmānuja's, was found praying to Viṣṇu standing among cowherd women. A disciple accosted him: "Why do you stand among these illiterate women instead of among Vaiṣṇava bhaktas?" Nampi answered, "Lord's grace flows over these illiterate cowherds as water flows from a higher to a lower level." The disciple asked, "How did they pray? How did your grace pray?" Nampi said, "They prayed to the Lord in pure Tamil. They said, 'Please drink this milk, eat this fruit. Live a hundred years. Wear this silk uppercloth.' I prayed in Sanskrit: 'Be victorious, be victorious.' " The other man said, "You couldn't forget your rough-sounding Sanskrit even among the cowherds. It looks as if we will be the same wherever we are." (Adapted from Venkatachari, pp. 43-44.)

tenth century,[30] and the bhakti works of the Vīraśaiva saints follow soon after in the eleventh and twelfth centuries. Chronologically, Marathi, close neighbor of Kannada, becomes the next venue for bhakti. And the cases of Gujerati (12th century), Kashmiri (14th century), Assamese (14-15th century), Oriya (15th century), Maithili (14th century), Braj (16th century), Avadhi (16th century), seem to bear out this relation between language development and bhakti.

A spoken dialect may, at a certain point, acquire the name and status of a "language." After all, a "language" is but a dialect with an army—and a poet.[31] In medieval India, vernaculars run true to this pattern. A language, once a mere dialect, becomes associated with courts and bards and begins to rival Sanskrit as a literary medium. One of its first written compositions is a bhakti work—which, in turn, asserts its importance as a new medium.

Even classical Tamil poetry reworks oral folk materials. Many genres, especially epics and bhakti poems, blend Sanskrit and Tamil traditions, and within Tamil, bridge the "high" and the "low." Bhakti poems are often written in folk meters, modelled on folk genres: good examples are Periyāḻvār's lullabies with *tā lē lō* refrains, poems on Kṛṣṇa's pot-dances (Tamil *kuṭamāṭikūttaṉ*), songs that accompany games like *ammāṉai* (jacks) and *untipaṟa* (a game of tag or toss). All these refrains, dances, and games are part of Tamil folklore to this day. The pounding "Pestle Songs" in

[30] Written material in Kannada dates from at least the 6th century A.D. In Bengali, although the Buddhist *caryāpadas* appear in the 10th century or so, Muslim invasions interrupt literary activity until the 14th century.

[31] The late Uriel Weinreich is credited with the epigram: "a language is a dialect with an army."

Māṇikkavācakar, the three-line (*tripadi*) metric bases of the Vīraśaiva vacanas (sayings), the many folk motifs in the Kannada dāsas (Vaiṣṇava poets) are other South Indian examples. The subject merits further exploration.[32]

Bhakti poets often contrast their language with Sanskrit, the "perfected language." To the "culture language" of Sanskrit they oppose their own "language of nature," and they insist on their self-images as persons of wild, untutored, spontaneous passion. In the āḻvār poem quoted on p. 119, "mumbling and prattling the many names of the Lord" is implicitly preferred to the careful, tutored, rote-learned enunciation of Sanskrit mantras. Basavaṇṇa, the Kannada Vīraśaiva saint (12th century) says,

> I don't know anything like time beats and metre
> nor the arithmetic of strings and drums;
> I don't know the count of iamb and dactyl.
>
> My lord of the meeting rivers,
> as nothing will hurt you
> I'll sing as I love.[33]

"Sanskrit is standing water, bhāṣā (vernacular) is flowing water," said Kabīr, the Hindi saint-poet (15th-16th century). A medieval commentator reverses the usual snobbery regarding Sanskrit as the language of the gods. The Tamil work *Tiruvāymoḻi*, he says, can be read by all; it is like a golden vessel that cannot be polluted by anyone's touch, whereas Sanskrit is a clay vessel that will be polluted by the touch of all and sun-

[32] See Lynn M. Ate, "Periyāḻvār's 'Tirumoḻi'—a Bāla Kṛṣṇa Text from the Devotional Period in Tamil Literature," and Norman Cutler, "The Poetry of the Tamil Saints," for beginnings in this direction.

[33] Ramanujan, *Speaking of Śiva*, p. 82.

dry. A seventeenth-century Śaiva writer praises Māṇikkavācakar's *Tiruvācakam* thus:

We have not seen hearts melt
  and eyes flow with tears
  when people read the Vedas,
but when they read the *Tiruvācakam*
  even once, black stony hearts will melt
  and tears will flow
    as from springs in the sands.

Kampaṉ, the Tamil epic poet (12th century), praises Nammāḻvār and the way the divine follows, rather than precedes, his poetry:

That first of flames,
  the flame of flames, . . .

it runs *before* the Vedas
  but it runs *after*
    any single line
    of our good poet
      whose mind's a sea.[34]

We may remember that, in temple processions, the singers of the Tamil hymns walk before the Lord's image, and the Vedic chanters follow after. Nammāḻvār himself says, in 7.8.10,

You are what they said
  in the Good Old Books:
"Than this
  there is nothing more subtle"

[34] *Ācāryahṛdayam*, 13th century, cū. 13. The next two verse passages are cited in Te. Po. Mīṉāṭcicuntaraṉār's Tamil work *Kulacēkarar* (Kōvai Kalaikkatir, 1961), pp. 5-6. The 17th-century Śaiva writer is Civavākkiyar.

you are that form
  and that formlessness

everlasting
  you wear lotus and basil
    on your chest

and whenever we say
  whatever we can
    it becomes you

however we say it

In such a poem, the Vedas, the "Good Old Books,"[35] are not rejected but placed: they are seen as one way of speaking about god, but not the only way. For whatever one says of the Lord, it fits, it "becomes" the Lord. In this verse, characteristic of the āḻvār, the language is positive, the Lord is not spoken of in terms of "not this, not that" (*neti neti*); he is not seen as beyond language, as "ineffable" (*anirvacanīya*); his infinite manifold accommodates itself to any language whatsoever. He is the subject of all predicates.

So we have here a religious poetry composed in a first language (in Tamil at this time, later in others). A first language is continuous with the language of one's earliest childhood and family, one's local folk and folklore. Sanskrit was probably never a first language in this sense.[36] As a second language, it was a language of

[35] A playful translation of the phrase *tollai naṉṉūl*, "the old good books."

[36] Van Buitenen, p. 37. The "eternal" "pan-Indian" character of Sanskrit (and the "great" tradition) needs qualification. As Staal rightly points out, Sanskritic cultural forms, like any other, are regional in origin: the oldest Vedic literature originated in the northwest, and Advaita philosophy probably in Kerala. The pronunciation of Sanskrit too is not unchanging or a-geographic—though it is claimed to be; studies of Vedic recitation have shown distinct

culture, an interprovincial lingua franca, preserver and carrier of traditions. Tradition envisioned it as nonlocal, translocal, a language not subject to "nature" or to the same vagaries of speech and change as a widely and communally spoken first language would be. A mother tongue changes from speaker to speaker, class to class, region to region; it changes even with the speaker's life stages. The word *saṃskṛta*, Sanskrit, means, "remade, cultured, perfected, confected." W. B. Yeats's magnificent stanza in "Sailing to Byzantium" speaks eloquently and precisely for classical Sanskrit:

> Once out of nature I shall never take
> My bodily form from any natural thing,
> But such a form as Grecian goldsmiths make

---

developments in Kerala (cf. J. F. Staal, *Nambudiri Veda Recitation*, The Hague: Mouton, 1961). Still, in popular as well as in learned conception, Sanskrit is "unchanging," "pan-Indian"—it is taught and learned as such. A timeless standardization is its essence and definition. Whatever the origins and careers of particular items, the Vedas, etc., are no longer identified regionally. It was also "pan-Indian" in the obvious sense it was interregional. (The parallels with English in modern India are noteworthy.) See also Daniel H.H. Ingalls, *An Anthology of Sanskrit Court Poetry*, p. 6, on the "artificial" character of Sanskrit: "As a general rule Sanskrit was not a language of the family. It furnished no subconscious symbols for the impressions which we receive in childhood nor for the emotions which form our character in early adolescence. Sanskrit was therefore divorced from an area of life whence the poetry of what I would call the natural language derives much of its strength."

We need to add that even first languages inevitably develop "artificial," poetic, technical sublanguages. What we call "natural" or "artificial" points to degrees of inwardness; and it can also be a matter of ideology. Such matters make for different kinds of poetry and poetics. In their effort to return to nature, in search of the real language of men, poets renew the language of their tribe—though they may never truly return to nature. See later section, "A new poetics?" pp. 161-164.

Of hammered gold and gold enamelling
To keep a drowsy emperor awake;
Or set upon a golden bough to sing
To lords and ladies of Byzantium
Of what is past, or passing, or to come.[37]

Conceived as timeless in a world of change and trivia, the best that was thought and known was supposed to be created, or archived, in Sanskrit for all times and all places.

Sanskrit, by its existence, expressed and confirmed a social organization of tradition that depended on a dichotomy between "great," pan-Indian elite traditions and many local, "little," vernacular traditions, with bilingual mediators between them.

In Sanskrit plays, women and servants spoke, not Sanskrit, but one of the Prakrits. As we know, the court poetry of the Gupta times was composed in Sanskrit; their imperial coins were indeed gold, but the Chinese pilgrim[38] found only barter systems and cowrie-shell coins in the villages.

"A Local Habitation and a Name"

By the sixth century, the Sanskrit texts themselves had been classified according to origin and audience as *śruti*

[37] "Sailing to Byzantium" in W. B. Yeats, *The Collected Poems of W. B. Yeats*, p. 217. It is not surprising that one of the sources of this much-discussed stanza is a Sanskrit text: "As a goldsmith takes the gold from an old piece of jewelry and shapes it into a more modern piece, so the self forgets the old body, takes hold of another body, whether like that of the fathers, or of the celestial singers . . . or of any other creature," *Bṛhadāraṇyaka Upaniṣad*, translated by Purohit Swami and Yeats, *The Ten Principal Upanishads*, pp. 155-56.

[38] The Chinese traveler is Fa-hsien. See Mookerji, p. 56.

and *smṛti*. *Śrutis* were esoteric, "revealed" scripture, the closed texts; the *smṛtis* were "remembered" texts, interpreted by experts, but open to all. The epics, the major Hindu mythologies (purāṇas), and the *Gītā* were such *smṛtis*; they were part of the direct bhakti inheritance.

In the first regional movements of bhakti, one hears a new kind of utterance that cannot be adequately described by earlier terms such as "heard, revealed" (*śruti*) or "remembered" (*smṛti*), or as "that which is known" (the Vedas), or as that which is learned by "sitting at or near the feet [of a teacher]" (the Upaniṣads). For, as the terms suggest, they by now represent passive, receptive modes. Bhaktas prefer the active mode. Nammāḻvār's text is called *Tiru-vāy-moḻi*, "holy-mouth-word," or "divine utterance"; Māṇikkavācakar called his work *Tiruvācakam*, "the holy utterance"; the Kannada-speaking Vīraśaivas called their poems *vacanas* or "sayings." The emphasis has shifted from hearing to speaking, from watching to dancing, from a passive to an active mode; from a religion and a poetry of the esoteric few to a religion and a poetry of anyone who can speak. This shift is paralleled by other religious shifts: from the noniconic to the iconic; from the nonlocal to the local; from the sacrificial-fire rituals (*yajña* and *homa*) meant to be performed only by Vedic experts to worship (*pūjā*) by nearly all; from rituals in which a plot of ground is temporarily cordoned off and made into sacred space by experts in a consecration rite—to worship in temples, localized, named, open to almost the whole range of Hindu society. These changes are accompanied by a shift away from the absolute godhead, the non-personal Brahman of the Upaniṣads, to the gods of the mythologies, with faces, complexions, families, feelings, personalities, characters. Bhakti poems celebrate god both as local and translocal, and especially as the nexus of the two. As the Murukaṉ poem (p. 115) says, he is the kind who dwells "here, but not only here." The poems celebrate the giving and the receiving, the reciprocity of human and divine.

One must add that bhakti traditions did not entirely discard Upaniṣadic concepts of a non-local, non-concrete godhead. Temples and images were seen by some as the earlier and inferior stages in the path of salvation; the ignorant may need images as props to lean on, but will soon leave them behind to move on to more abstract stages. A distinction is made between a god "with attributes" (*saguṇa*) and a god "without attributes" (*nirguṇa*).[39] A prayer attributed to Śaṃkara points up the paradox:

O lord, forgive me my three human sins:
you are everywhere, yet I worship you here;
you are without form, yet I worship you
in these, and these other forms;
you need no praise, yet I offer you
this prayer.
Lord, forgive me my three human sins.

But the āḻvār's god is never *nirguṇa*, attributeless, never without "body, parts, or passion," or without a local habitation and a name. The saint does not see god's attributes as human, all-too-human, attributions or projections; nor are the attributes, when given, only the "good" ones.

[39] *Saguṇa/nirguṇa* contrasts in bhakti can be overdone. A bhakti poet of either school attends to the tension or oscillation between the two aspects of god. See note in Dimock, et al. *The Literatures of India*, p. 70. That this paradoxical prayer should be attributed to the monist Śaṃkara is a recognition of the tension.

Being all three worlds
  and nothing

being desire
  being rage
being both the flower-born Lakṣmī
  and anti-Lakṣmī
    black goddess of ill-luck

being both honor and shame

our lord
  lives in Viṇṇakar
    city named Sky
which the gods worship lovingly

and in my evil heart
he lives forever
  flame of flames.

Nammāḻvār, 6.3.6

God, the pervasive Absolute, is in all dual opposites. *Muraṇ*, perversity, a naughty contrariness, is one of his attributes. By paradox and contrast, he "teases thought into eternity." He is the principle of continuity between opposites and differences. God out there in the universe is also in the temple as he is in the devotee's heart. He is at once the other, the indweller, and the icon. Like one's mother tongue, he is everywhere, accessible. He is one's own thoughts (1.8.7, p. 50).

To Nammāḻvār, god is not a hieratic second language, a Sanskrit to be learned, to be minded lest one forget its rules, paradigms, and exceptions; he is one's own mother tongue. In his view, god lives inside us as a mother tongue does, and we live in god as we live in language—a language that was there before us, is all around us in the community, and will be there after us. To lose this first language is to lose one's beginnings, one's bearings, to be exiled into aphasia. But then, he is both memory and loss of memory, both heaven and hell (7.8.6, p. 20).

Thus the early poet-saints required and created a poetry and a poetics of the mother tongue. Their self-image did not permit the poetry or poetics of a learned, courtly tradition, a scriptural or decorous language apart from oneself, an art that one masters and elaborates with care and anxiety, and never with any complete confidence. Unlike the mother tongue, Sanskrit is the language of the fathers.[40] One takes no liberties with it; in it, one aspires to an artistry of "ornament" and "essence" (*alaṃkāra* and *rasa*)—an "artifice of eternity," in Yeats's phrase.

In the saints' poetry, the language is often dialectal; often the saints do not consider themselves poets at all. The relations with god are the familiar dyadic ones, in which one shares a language with the Other: as servant and master, protégé and protector, beloved and lover, child and mother.[41]

[40] See Fr. Walter J. Ong's (jaw-breaking yet relevant) remarks on Latin: "By around A.D. 550-700, Latin was settling down as a chirographically controlled language, thereafter fated normally to be acquired extradomestically in all-male schools by boys previously acquainted with speech in at least one other tongue. Latin was never more learned by in-fantes, non-speakers. . . . Latin was distance-alienated—not from day-to-day life, for it was the substance of daily life for lawyers, physicians, academic educators, and clergymen, but from the psychological and psychosomatic roots of consciousness. It no longer in any sense belonged to mother. It did not come from where you came from." Other learned languages with similar developments are, of course, Sanskrit, Classical Chinese, Classical Arabic, and Rabbinic Hebrew. One must add, for balance, that these "father-tongues" "have been of the utmost importance for the development of thought and civilization—during their ascendance much more important than any mother tongues." Ong, *Interfaces of the Word*, pp. 27-28.

[41] Piḷḷai Lokācārya (13th century) speaks of nine kinds of intimate

Not only is he familiar as a mother tongue; he is a familiar figure, like a local Tamil chieftain and playboy—powerful yet accessible. As a devotee, the āḻvār is the girl next-door. She teases him; he teases her in turn. She falls for him and feels tormented by jealousy when he takes up with other women. The dialogue is conducted in familiar colloquial tones.

Don't tell us those lies,

heaven and earth
    know your tricks.

Just one thing,
  my lord of the ancient wheel
      that turns at your slightest wish:

while all those girls
    —their words pure honey—
stand there
    wilting for love of you,

don't playact here and sweet-talk
  our lisping mynahs,
      our chattering parrots!

6.2.5

Mutuality and Grace

In the logic of dyadic relationships (e.g., mother/child, god/devotee), the two terms are defined by each other;

---

dyadic relationships: those between father and son, protector and protégé, master and servant, husband and wife, the person who understands and the object that is understood, the owner and his property, body and soul, the thing that is dependent and the things on which it depends, the person who enjoys and the thing that is enjoyed. These nine kinds of relationship are interlinked. See Venkatachari, pp. 139-140.

they need and confirm each other, bound each to each. So one doesn't *earn* god's grace in the Nammāḻvār poems; it is always there, given in the very nature of the relation. The Lord's grace needs no cause (*nirhetuka*, as the commentators say), requires no struggle, only an occasion:

I just said,
  "The grove and hill of my lord,"

and he came down
  and filled my heart:

he usually lives
  in the city of names

south of the Kāvēri,
  river of diamonds.

10.8.1

Grace is "arbitrary," but not capricious (as it may seem to a Calvinist or a Vīraśaiva); gratuitous, given free; unearned, universal.[42]

Why would anyone want
  to learn anything by Rāma?

Beginning with the low grass
  and the creeping ant
with nothing
    whatever,

[42] Such a universal salvation seems (to me) to adapt a Jaina-like view—especially because it includes, compassionately, the low grass and the creeping ant. The difference, of course, lies in Jaina salvation (freedom from karma bonds) being automatic; here salvation does not happen by natural process, but by its opposite, grace. Not enough attention has been paid to the influence of Jaina thought and practice on South Indian bhakti—especially on Śaiva bhakti.

he took everything in his city,
  everything moving,
    everything still,

he took everything,
  everything born
of the lord
  of four faces,

he took them all
  to the very best of states.

7.5.1

The poem makes short work of the human struggle for salvation, and of special elective grace. Later commentators spoke of two contrasted attitudes to grace in a striking pair of metaphors: the cat's way and the monkey's way.[43] In the cat's way, god and devotee are related as a mother cat is to her kittens: the kittens do nothing, the mother picks them up by the scruff of their necks and moves them around. In the monkey's way, god is a mother monkey to her baby monkeys: the mother does nothing for them as she lopes indifferently from branch to branch, but the baby holds on to the leaping mother for dear life.[44] These contrasted attitudes, emphases, as well as differing valuations of Sanskrit and Tamil as religious languages, led to a theological schism within the Śrī Vaiṣṇava sects.[45]

[43] The cat's way and the monkey's way (*nyāya* or rule) as popular parables about god's grace and man's efforts to earn it seem to have no clear textual source.

[44] Note the conception of god as mother (whether cat or monkey). In love he is the young male, in one's ignorance the guru, in distress the friend, in times of danger the father, in grace he is the mother.

[45] The two rival sects, Teṅkalai ("southern") and Vaṭakalai ("northern"), emphasize—often in bitter polemic—different branches

Later theologians explore in detail one of the persistent moods in the hymns. For the āḻvārs, and for the later theologians, bhakti or devotion is not enough: *prapatti*[46] or surrender is the one thing needful. None of the three paths of the *Gītā*—devotion (*bhakti*), right knowledge (*jñāna*), right action or ritual (*karma*)—is enough. For each still relies on effort, on some kind of merit. None trusts in, relies on, the essential nature of the soul—which is to submit to god. But *prapatti* or surrender works for everyone, whatever be his state, status, caste, or previous history. Not merit, but demerit may qualify the soul for grace. Not learning or high caste, but their opposite may endear one to god. The Lord himself is both the means (*upāya*) and the goal (*upeya*). For *prapatti*, there are no conditions of place, time, manner, fitness. The only condition is that the Lord, and only the Lord, be the object. Draupadī,

---

of the guru lineage after Rāmānuja, and different aspects of the hymns and the commentaries. The theological ways begin to part in the 13th century with Vedāntadeśika and Piḷḷai Lokācārya. The differences are complex, though they often wear Pelagian faces and seem to rehearse the faith *vs* works arguments of Christian theology. For the so-called eighteen differences, see A. Govindacarya, "The Astadasa-bhedas." The rivalry and the hardening of differences became most acute after the 18th century with the growing struggle for administrative control over the temples. See Venkatachari pp. 165-66, Carman p. 212. For the legal battles, see Appadurai.

[46] *Prapatti*, from the Sanskrit *prapad* "to drop down, to take refuge with." *Śaraṇam*, *Śaraṇāgati* ("surrender") are also favorite words in the context. *Śaraṇam* (Tamil *caraṇ*) occurs often in Nammāḻvār. The word has Buddhist associations. One must add that words like *prapatti* are the focus of continuous controversy. See Vasudha Rajagopalan, "The Śrī Vaiṣṇava Understanding of Bhakti and Prapatti (from the āḻvārs to Vedānta Deśika)"; Carman, pp. 214-237.

the heroine of the *Mahābhārata*, performed *prapatti* when she was menstruating and unclean; Arjuna received the Lord's counsel and grace on the battlefield, surrounded by vile and unclean people.[47]

In Nammāḻvār, god is not distant. Bound to human causes, his compassion is ever ready to flow toward the devotee. Among the members of the *teṅkalai*, or southern, sect of Śrī Vaiṣṇavas, one is asked not even to worship too hard, for the Lord is a person of infinite feeling. A devotee once said to me, "Don't prostrate yourself more than thrice in his presence. Don't wring his heart, don't work on his feelings."[48] A gesture, a token, is enough.

Congregation

Service to earlier bhaktas is often valued more highly than direct service to god. Bhakti includes devotion to one's *guru* or *ācārya* ("teacher"). One of the āḻvārs is called *toṇṭaraṭippoṭi*, "the dust on the feet of the Lord's servants." A sense of congregation (*bhāgavatagoṣṭhi*), somewhat like the Buddhist sense of *saṅgha*, places the devotee, in time and in space, among like-minded others; makes him akin to his masters, his examples.

Would I, sinner that I am,
  rather enter the fragrance,
    the lotus feet
  of our lord,

  divine dwarf

[47] Adapted from Piḷḷai Lokācārya's *Śrīvacanabhūṣaṇam*. See Robert Lester, *Śrīvacana Bhūṣaṇa of Piḷḷai Lokācārya*.

[48] Taped interview with a Teṅkalai pundit, Śrī Narasiṃhācārya, Madurai, 1963.

making great his little body
till it overwhelms
all three worlds,

when my masters,
his great servants
who have taken on small
human lives,

are content to roam this world?

8.10.3

The poet invokes Vāmana, the divine dwarf, a favorite of the āḻvārs. Viṣṇu made himself small to become the dwarf. The motif of "his little greatness" (*cirumā*) is repeated and reversed: the Lord as dwarf expands, and overwhelms the worlds, and his great servants take on small human lives. The poem also attends to the lotus feet of the Lord; Vāmana measured the worlds with his feet and, with one foot on demon Bali's head, pressed him down into the netherworld. Feet are celebrated Buddhist motifs, and they receive a great deal of attention in bhakti. Devotees are called *aṭiyār*, "men at the feet"; the Vaiṣṇava word for the first person pronoun is "*aṭiyēṉ*" meaning "I, at your feet."

In their intense feeling for god and congregation, the saints envisage bhakti very differently from the *Gītā*, an earlier text which makes major use of the concept. For one thing, in the *Gītā* god speaks to man. Although Kṛṣṇa is compared to father, friend, lover,[49] he presents

[49] Arjuna, awe-struck, says, "How rashly have I called You comrade . . . distraught was I, or was it that I loved you?" 11.41. In 11.44, "Bear with me, I beg You, as father [bears] with son, or friend with friend, or lover with one he loves, O God!" Translated by Zaehner, pp. 316-17. Christian editors like Zaehner and post-Christian Hindu editors like Rādhakrishnan often interpret or translate certain Sanskrit words in the text as "love." For example, in

himself only as awesome Lord and omniscient guru. Nowhere does anything corresponding to the Tamil saints' *aṉpu* ("love") appear in the Sanskrit *Gītā* as a possible relation between man and god.

Furthermore, in the *Gītā*, the relation between god and man is a one-to-one relation. Salvation is individual, a "flight of the alone to the Alone." Each man, with his unique *karma*, is alone in his career and salvation. If one may indulge in diagrams, the diagram for the *Gītā* conception would look like this:

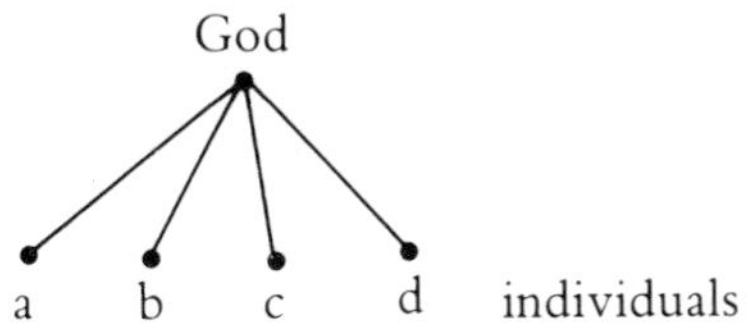

Contrast Buddhism: the initiates are bound to each other in a *saṅgha*, a community; all of them are related to the compassionate Buddha. In early conceptions, the Buddha was more guru than god. The Buddhist diagram would be:

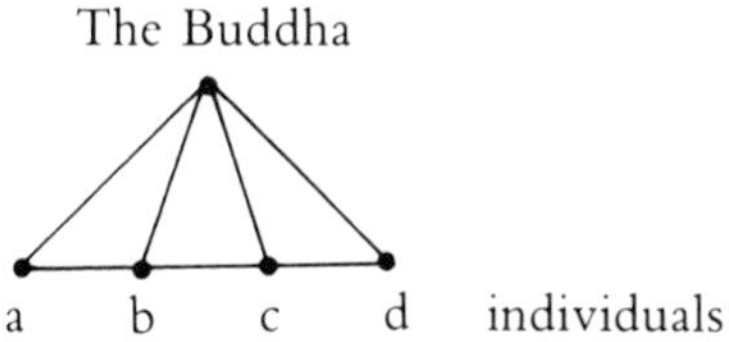

Three kinds of relations become real in bhakti movements. Each is envisioned as a body-soul or part-whole (*śarīra/śarīri*) relation. Devotees become members of a

12.14-20, "sa me *priyaḥ*" is read as "I love the man who . . . " instead of "he is dear to me, who . . ." Zaehner, pp. 329-31.

congregation—which, in turn, is related to a guru, or to a saint like Nammāḻvār, exemplar and forerunner. Directly, or indirectly through the guru figure, one worships the Lord and his local forms.

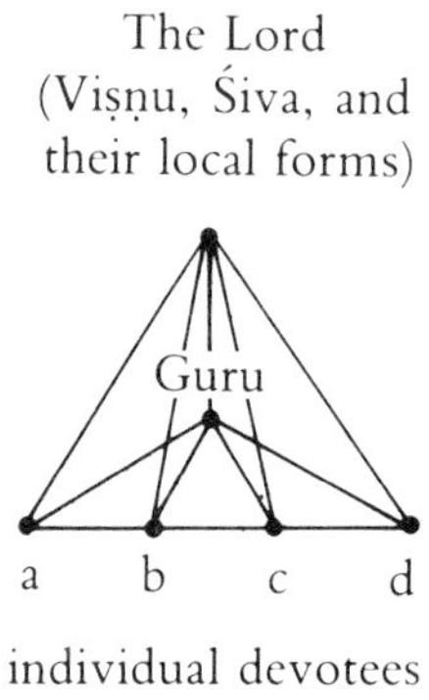

The whole congregation ripens together toward salvation; "in a bunch, one ripe banana warms and ripens all others." Devotees benefit even nondevotees: "if a field is well watered, the water seeps into the next field too."[50]

Being in Touch

The āḻvārs (and the nāyaṉmārs) thrive on contagion, communion in community, being in touch with each other. Nammāḻvār says that all five senses[51] are "the bodies of god" (1.9.9), and he strains all of them to

[50] The first comparison is from Tāyumāṉavar (Śaiva, 17th-18th century), the second from Piḷḷai Lokācārya's *Śrīvacanabhuṣaṇam*, sūtra 260.

[51] For the five senses as tormentors, see 7.1.6 (p. 37) in the same section.

realize god. Yet the sensory modes he favors in his poetry are the "near senses": touch, taste, smell.

The Vedic poets were "seers"; philosophy is a "seeing" (*darśana*); and the word "see" occurs in the *Gītā* scores of times.[52] The Vedas are "heard" (*śruti*), as earlier classical Tamil poems were "things heard" (*kēḷvi*). Both sight and hearing are senses of distance. But the favorite bhakti sense is the sense of touch; bhakti is contact, contagion. The devotee's heart or hands touch, not just the feet of god, but his entire body.

For the sake of that girl,
    her mouth red as a berry,
  you broke the seven bulls;

you bent the long bow
  and finished off the king
    of the island of towers;

and you broke the tusk
  of that pedigreed elephant.

I haven't worshiped you
  with flowers and holy water
    at proper times;

but then
  my heart is the only sandalwood
    to rub and perfume your body with,

your body
    dark as *kāyā*-blossom.

4.3.1

[52] Sensory modes, especially visual analogues of knowing, have received much attention in recent years. See Ong, *Interfaces of the Word*, and his other works. "Seeing" is a metaphor for "knowing" in the *Gītā*: Zaehner p. 156. Note, in English (Indo-European) usage: seer, insight, outlook, vision, scope, speculate, etc.

In anthropological terms, Hindu society is structured through caste, with rules governing exchanges; the Hindu is (notoriously) homo hierarchicus. Taboo, non-touching, defines the boundaries between categories. But bhakti depends on *mana*, touching, merging.[53] In some forms of bhakti, breaking the taboos on touch and pollution becomes quite central. For instance, the taboo on pollution forbids any food touched or eaten by specified others. Such leftover food is shunned as "*eccil*" in Tamil, "*eñjalu*" in Kannada (both meaning "saliva"). But Basavaṇṇa, the Kannada saint, offers it to god:

> Milk is left over
> from the calves.
>
> Water is left over
> from the fishes,
> flowers from the bees.
>
> How can I worship you,
> O Śiva, with such offal?
> But it's not for me
> to despise leftovers,
> so take what comes,
>
> lord of the meeting rivers.[54]

Vaiṣṇavas love to tell the story of Śabarī in the *Rāmāyaṇa.* Śabarī, an old low-caste woman devoted to Rāma, waits years for him to appear. When he does appear, she feeds him fresh fruit from her tree, but not before she has lovingly tasted them all herself—for she wishes to offer him only the ripest and the sweetest.

[53] On "mana" and "taboo," see Anthony F. C. Wallace, *Religion: An Anthropological View*, pp. 60-61.

[54] Ramanujan, *Speaking of Śiva*, p. 90.

Such an act would violate every rule of worship and honor, for no food already tasted or flower once worn[55] may be offered to a god; in a brahman household, all food is first offered to a god, then received back as leftovers to be eaten by the family.

In later bhakti cults,[56] this impulse to touch and merge results, however briefly and often only in theory, in a breakdown of barriers and distinctions between caste and caste, between touchable and untouchable, between male and female; it also neutralizes any distinctions between sacred and profane in time and space.

Nammāḻvār is reputed to be a farmer (*veḷḷāḷa*) by birth, but he is the most revered of the āḻvār saints.

The four castes
  uphold all clans;
go down, far down
  to the lowliest outcastes
    of outcastes:

[55] Āṇṭāḷ (9th century) the Vaiṣṇava woman-saint, was called "cūṭik-koṭutta-nācciyār," "the lady who gave (flowers to god) after wearing (them)." She is said to have worn flowers in her hair, dreaming of love for the divine lover Kṛṣṇa, and to have sent them in the morning to the temple—where the sacrilege was discovered. In love poetry, lovers eat from one another's mouths; intimacy breaks the taboo. Giving god one's leftovers is to treat him as a lover.

[56] Early bhakti poetry like that of the āḻvārs and the nāyaṉmārs, and the poetry of later movements like that of the Vīraśaivas (10th-12th century), or of Kabīr or Caitanya, are in many ways strikingly different from each other. Bhakti is often treated as all of one piece; the varieties of bhakti, certain differences between early and late, Śaiva and Vaiṣṇava, male and female, the "manic" and the "depressive," are yet to be precisely described.

if they are the intimate henchmen
  of our lord
    with the wheel in his right hand,
    his body dark as blue sapphire,

then even the slaves of their slaves
  are our masters.

3.7.9

The social world is still seen as a hierarchy, but as one ordered by men's relation to god, not by birth. The array of lord and servant, of servant below servant, a Hindu root metaphor,[57] is maintained but in reverse.

"Mutual Cannibalism"

Another, rather drastic, way of partaking or merging is to devour the other:

My dark one
  stands there as if nothing's
            changed

after taking entire
into his maw
  all three worlds
    the gods
    and the good kings
who hold their lands

[57] Inden's phrase, in Ronald Inden, "Lordship and Caste in Hindu Discourse," p. 3. According to Inden, during the period from the 8th to the 12th century, "the makers of Vaiṣṇava and Śaiva discourse . . . constructed worlds that were populated with lords seemingly endless in their variety. . . . Every conceivable category of thing, place, animal, and person had its lord."

as a mother would
  a child in her womb—

and I
  by his leave
  have taken him entire

and I hold him in my belly
for keeps

9.6.10

The poem plays with the container and the contained. The Lord who devoured the worlds, and Kṛṣṇa who ate mud and showed his mother the fourteen worlds in his mouth including herself, and the Kṛṣṇa of the *Gītā* who showed his universal form (*viśvarūpa*) as containing all things, are favored parallels in this kind of discourse. The Lord is *antaryāmī*, the controller within, the indweller; and he contains other containers (worlds, kings, mothers). The devotee is within him, and he is within the devotee. In 9.6.10, with its image of mutual physical cannibalism, the reciprocity is carried all the way; the eater is eaten, the container is contained, in a metonymy many times over.

This cluster of motifs appears variously in myth, ritual, and legend.[58] In the brahman initiation ritual (*upa-*

[58] S. A. Dange, *Legends in the Mahabharata*, pp. 155-237. Sage Mārkaṇḍeya is swallowed by Viṣṇu, roams inside his belly, slips outside, and is terrified by the ocean and the world in darkness and by Viṣṇu's sleeping form. Viṣṇu swallows him again, and Mārkaṇḍeya back in his belly thought his vision a dream. Dimmitt and van Buitenen pp. 253-56. Recently, O'Flaherty ("Inside and Outside the Mouth of God: The Boundary between Myth and Reality," p. 97) has suggested that the swallowing god is female. Śiva swallows the demonic sage Śukra and emits him through his phallus; Śukra in turn swallows the divine sage Kaca and emits *him* through his side. "Each of these sages emerges with the secret of

nayana), the preceptor symbolically swallows and disgorges the initiate, who thereby gains new life and becomes "twice-born." In Vedic mythology, the cosmic enemies Indra and Vṛtra swallow each other, as sun and moon do in eclipse myths. The cluster pertains to initiation, consecration, the drinking of Soma and the attainment of immortality, and the sacrifice as the embryo in the womb—a pattern of engulfment, death, and rejuvenation. The eater and the eaten are equal in power (or powerlessness); they alternate between oneness and separateness, as god and devotee.

In myths these events happen to others. But in these poems, they happen to the speaker himself and develop new meanings—like reciprocity, a contest of intimacy, a wrestling for who would contain whom first. A certain glee and humor play on what would otherwise be horrendous events.

9.6.10 is the last poem of a decad that explores the mutual cannibalism of god and devotee; these ten poems are considered by commentators as "the very life of the great Thousand Verses" of Nammāḻvār.

God as Lover

The most passionate touching and partaking of another, or the need to do so, is in the erotic/sexual re-

---

immortality and is, in addition, made immortal by becoming the child of the god who gives birth to him." See note 44 on god the mother. In European mystical literature, see: "To eat and be eaten! this is union! Since His desire is without measure, to be devoured by Him does not greatly amaze me." Ruysbroeck (Flemish mystic, 14th century), quoted in Evelyn Underhill, *Mysticism*, p. 425.

lation. One meaning of *bhaj* (the verb root in *bhakti*) is to share a body, to copulate, to unite.[59]

Writers on mysticism have written a great deal about love as a metaphor in the world's traditions.[60] Both the Vedas and the Upaniṣads speak, though not often, in such metaphors. The *Bṛhadāraṇyaka Upaniṣad* (4.2.21) likens union with the Self to a sexual embrace: "Just as a man fully embraced by his beloved wife does not know anything at all, either external or internal, so does this man, embraced fully by the supremely knowing spiritual self (*prajñātman*), not know anything at all, either external or internal."[61]

According to Sānkhya-Yoga philosophy, a passive male principle (*puruṣa*) and an active female energy (*prakṛti*) unite to create the universe. Hindu esoteric schools of tantra enact a similar allegory in a sexual ritual; Buddhist tantra reverses the male-female roles. Yet these are only analogies; for even in the sexual ritual, human love or any form of relationship between the partners is rejected.[62] But in bhakti, the relationship is everything. In the āḻvār poems, the figure of speech, the as-if of erotic allegory, becomes the here-and-now of dramatic poems.

In a story often cited, 60,000 sages want to become united with Viṣṇu in his incarnation as Rāma. Rāma tells the sages that he cannot oblige them in his present role, for as Rāma he is sworn to monogamy. But he will oblige them in his next incarnation as Kṛṣṇa; the sages can all be reborn as cowherd women (*gopis*) and

[59] See note 2 on the meanings of *bhaj*.

[60] Underhill.

[61] Translated by Hume, *The Thirteen Principal Upaniṣads*, p. 136.

[62] Charlotte Vaudeville, "Evolution of Love Symbolism in Bhagavatism," p. 32.

unite with him in love. In this view, all devotees are felt to be feminine; the Lord is the supreme male, the lover.

In the āḻvār's poems, for the first time in the history of Indian literature, the Kṛṣṇa myth provides a full scenario for present action and poetry; the poet enacts it, relives it in many roles. A myth becomes a correlative for present feeling; a cultural archetype is invoked by and for present experience. Nammāḻvār devotes twenty-seven decads, or 270 poems, in *Tiruvāymoḻi* and all the 100 poems of *Tiruviruttam* to the theme of love. In these, he speaks as an actor in the Kṛṣṇa myth; he is the beloved who pines for the Lord, sends birds as messengers to him, sees all nature pining for him; the poet is also the girlfriend who consoles and counsels, and the mother who restrains her and despairs over her daughter's love-sick fantasies. The āḻvār speaks in many feminine roles—as women in love, mothers, girlfriends—in voices made famous by classical Tamil poetry.

The love poems alternate with other kinds of poems. The thirteenth-century commentary, *Ācāryahṛdayam*, explains this alternation: "In knowledge, his own words; in love, a woman's words."[63] Yet knowledge (*ñānam*, Sanskrit *jñāna*) and love (*prēmam*) interpenetrate, as in 5.6.5 below.

The poet's many themes, philosophy, mythology, the experience of possession, merge in a complex love poem, as a mother watches her daughter's crazy moods of love for her god:

[63] *Ācāryahṛdayam*, "The Master's Heart," by Aḻakiyamaṇavāḷa Nāyaṉār, is a commentary in Sanskritized Tamil (*maṇipravāḷa*) in 234 sections.

My daughter says,
"Unfailing, I guard the earth."

"Unfailing, I lifted the mountain," says she,
"slew the demons,
taught strategems to the Five Brothers
once upon a time."

"Unfailing, I churned the ocean," says she.

Can it be that the unfailing lord,
his body dark as the sea,
has taken her over?

Good words fail
with my daughter now,

how can I tell you,
successful men of the world?

5.6.5

A mother's bewilderment frames and questions the experience: does the daughter speak as a god? is she merely crazy? has the god possessed her, and have the two become one? has she taken on his powers?

God-lover, beloved, watching mother, and sceptical worldlings coexist and interact within the poem: the poet in his many parts can speak at once of the girl's craziness, the lovers' oneness, as well as of the wonderment and doubt at such oneness. They also represent different stages of the bhakti career. One does not need to allegorize the poem[64] to see that it is at once a philosophic and a love poem.

[64] The *Ācāryahṛdayam*, for instance, finds inner meanings (*svāpadeśam*) allegorizing every detail of Nammāḻvār's love poems. For instance, the mother, the friend, and the woman in love are seen as

Another difference between the Upaniṣadic passage (p. 00) and the āḻvār poems must be noted. The love poems express a range of feelings, but most of them are preoccupied with absence, not presence, not the bliss of union but the pain of separation; they convey what is called *viraha* in Sanskrit, *mullai* and *neytal*[65] in Tamil poetics.

The distinction parallels the central theological one between the Lord's otherness (*paratva*) and his easy accessibility (*saulabhya*)[66]—a distinction that characterizes

---

three stages of knowledge: the firm knowledge that allows one to wait for god, the knowledge of the relation between soul and god, and the heart's knowledge that makes the devotee hasten to experience him. Even the various parts of the beloved's body are allegorized: the red lips are "desire" (*rāga* "red, desire"), the full breast called "vessel" (*ceppu*) is bhakti that makes one fit for god's enjoyment, etc. Similarly, night is false knowledge. The love's messenger birds are the teachers (*ācāryas*) who relate the soul to god.

It is ironic that while the poems make the abstract concrete, the commentary undoes the poem by reversing the direction. The poem is public yet experiential; the commentary here makes it esoteric, technical.

[65] *Mullai* is the lover's mood of patient waiting for the absent one, set in a forest or pastoral landscape; *neytal*, set in the seashore, is the mood of anxious waiting. For details, Ramanujan, *The Interior Landscape*. I am indebted to Friedhelm Hardy for a personal communication on this theme in Nammāḻvār.

[66] *Paratva/saulabhya*: see p. 124. Commentators favor two examples above all of the Lord's accessibility: of all the *avatāras* or descents of the god in answer to human need, Kṛṣṇa is the most accessible. He plays pranks, steals butter, allows himself to be tied to a millstone; later he becomes Arjuna's charioteer and helps the Pāṇḍavas win their battles. The other instance is the Lord's presence in hundreds of local temple images (*arca*). Piḷḷai Lokācārya says: "Setting aside his completeness and his self-sufficiency, he appears here, caring even for those who do not care for him." (Lester, p. 23, translation mine.) "Being free, He becomes bound, being in-

the āḻvārs' deepest experience of all being: its nearness coupled with its mysterious otherness, its unavailability. The latter makes the former precious, precarious, a thing of grace.

Dear friend,
  dear as the Dark One's paradise:

night grows long, many lives long,
  when we part;
or goes fast, a split second many times split,
  when we are together.

So I suffer even when my lover joins me
  many nights in a row,
and suffer again
  when he goes away.

Blessed night, ever flowing,
  is full of tricks,
  plays fast and loose.

Tiruviruttam 16

The otherness is a condition of grace. So is separation a condition for bhakti. The poet exults in union, intimacy, *saulabhya*, not in the love poems, but in poems of what I have called possession, cannibalism and take-over in earlier sections.

The "Signifiers" of Bhakti

Not only the personae, but the landscapes and the situations of classical Tamil love poetry (and heroic po-

---

dependent, He becomes dependent for all His service on His devotee." Quoted by Bharatan Kumarappa, *The Hindu Conception of Deity as Culminating in Rāmānuja*, p. 316.

etry) are enlisted as "signifiers" for a new "signification." Let us compare a classical Tamil poem with one of Nammāḻvār's:

What Her Girl-friend Said

These fat *koṉṟai* trees
are gullible:

the season of rains
that he spoke of
when he went through the stones
of the desert
is not yet here

though these trees
mistaking the untimely rains
have put out
their long arrangements of flowers
on the twigs

as if for a proper monsoon.
Kōvatattaṉ, *Kuṟuntokai* 66

Nammāḻvār follows the classical score closely, yet transposes it to a new key:

What Her Girl-friend Said

They haven't flowered yet,
the fat *koṉṟai* trees,
nor hung out their garlands
and golden circlets
in their sensual canopy of leaves
along the branches,

dear girl,
dear as the paradise of our lord
who measured the earth
girdled by the restless sea:

they are waiting
with buds
for the return
of your lover
  once twined in your arms.
    Tiruviruttam 68

The changes are subtle. The trees, like all of nature, like the beloved and the speaker herself, are waiting for the rain, haven't flowered yet. The second verse introduces, though only parenthetically, Viṣṇu who measured the earth. We know from other poems he is the lover, the Dark One dark as the raincloud. With him in the middle of it, the rain resonates with new meanings.

The waiting for reunion, the imminence of a monsoon about to burst, the flowers yet in bud, are all qualified by the phrase "dear girl, dear as the paradise (*vaikuṇṭam*) of our lord." For the Lord's return to his paradise is natural, certain. The āḻvār, like paradise, is the favorite dwelling place of Viṣṇu.

Sometimes, a single epithet or name such as the "Dark One" makes all the difference (e.g., 9.9.10, p. 33). Sometimes nothing *in* the love poem, only the company it keeps, makes one search for religious, "symbolic" meanings.[67] Just as a divine name, or the company of saints is said to change a man into a bhakta, so too a name or a context can change a "profane" poem into a "sacred" one (e.g., 1.4.8, p. 52).

Or, we can speak of "framing" the erotic poem, in a new context of bhakti. In *Tiruviruttam* 68 above, the "framing" is achieved by the presence of a reference to "paradise" and to the "lord who measured the earth."

[67] See *Song of Songs*, among the books of the Bible, and the controversy about its meanings.

Any sign is a union of signifier and signified. In earlier poetry, the flowering tree, the rain, the anxious beloved, and so forth, were the signifiers for the erotic mood of waiting (*mullai*). In Nammāḻvār's poem, the entire erotic tradition has become a new signifier, with bhakti as the signified. The classical tradition is to bhakti what the erotic motifs are to the tradition. This transposition can be diagrammed thus:[68]

<table>
<tr><td>SIGNIFIER$_1$
(rain, flowering tree, etc.)</td><td>SIGNIFIED$_1$
(the erotic mood/*akam*)</td><td></td></tr>
<tr><td colspan="2">SIGNIFIER$_2$
(the entire erotic tradition)</td><td>SIGNIFIED$_2$
(bhakti)</td></tr>
</table>

Past traditions and borrowings are thus reworked into bhakti; they become materials, signifiers for a new signification—as a bicycle seat becomes a bull's head in Picasso. Often, the listener/reader moves between the original material and the work before him—the double vision is part of the poetic effect.

The signifiers for bhakti come from a wide range of earlier, even ready-made traditions, conventions, and concepts. A list of such signifiers would also serve as a summary of what we have said so far:

1. Vedic/Upaniṣadic concepts and symbols
2. Buddhist (and Jaina) elements

[68] See Roland Barthes, *Elements of Semiology*, pp. 89-90, on "staggered systems," especially the diagram for connotation that I follow here.

3. Purāṇa mythologies
4. Love poetry and heroic poetry in Tamil (or Sanskrit poetry, for later bhakti, and in other regions)
5. Earlier notions of bhakti from the *Gītā*, *Paripāṭal* and *Tirumurukāṟṟuppaṭai*
6. Folk religion, folk meters, motifs, and genres

A New Poetics?

In the course of these transpositions, the poetry and the poetics become strikingly different from anything in earlier Tamil or Sanskrit, in the following ways:

1. The speaker, the worshiper, is always in sight. This is never the case in classical love poetry, which is an impersonal poetry of personae. The classical poems are framed as dramatic monologues. In the āḻvār poems, even the classical personae (lover, beloved, etc.) are rendered personal; they express the āḻvār's relation to his god-lover. The poet and speaker are one.

2. *Rasa* poetry (not confined to Sanskrit) aims at *rasa*[69] or aesthetic emotion, "emotion recollected," experience generalized and depersonalized by means of a

[69] *Rasa* ("sap/essence") is the Sanskrit technical term for aesthetic experience. *Rasa* is aesthetic emotion; *bhāva* is "natural" human feeling. The *rasa* exists or is produced from a combination (of its elements. . . .) *vibhāvas* "causes of emotion, e.g., the persons and circumstances represented," *anubhāvas* "effects, consequences, or external signs of emotions," and *vyabhicarībhāvas* "transitory states (of mind)." Bharata, quoted in Edwin Gerow, *Indian Poetics*, p. 249. We may think of *rasa* and its components semiotically as "signified" and "signifier."

In the terminology of *rasa*, bhakti is a new *rasa* that uses other *rasas* (like the erotic or heroic) as *bhāvas*. Needless to say, neither *rasa* nor *bhakti* poetics guarantees good poems: they only speak of different biases and different kinds of poems.

structure, a poesis, a making. In bhakti poems, such a *rasa* is no longer the end (though it may be the result, especially when we look at the poems as "texts"). In them *bhāva* "feeling," *anubhava* "experience," are much-prized terms. We have here a poetics of *bhāva*, not *rasa*, a poetics of personal feeling whether aesthetic or not. As the poet is entirely given to his god, he believes in a spontaneity that is also possession. The title *Tiruvāymoḻi* can be read two ways: as *tiruvāy-moḻi* "word of holy mouth," or as *tiru-vāymoḻi* "holy word-of-mouth." The poet's words are his own and his god's; his poetics are a poetics of possession (see 10.7.1, p. 76).

3. *Rasa* poetics depends on a number of distinctions. The poet, his subject and his characters, the player and his role in the play, the emotions within poetry and outside poetry, and finally, the players and the audience are all carefully distinguished. Poeticians[70] insist that the Kṛṣṇa in a play is not to be identified with the author, nor with the Kṛṣṇa of the myths, nor with the actor playing Kṛṣṇa. Nor should any member of the audience identify with him. He is a *virtual* presence in poetic, not in actual, space. *Rasa* depends on aesthetic distance. But in the poetics of bhakti, these distinctions are blurred, if not anulled. The Lord (the subject of the poem) becomes the poet. The roles in a mythic narrative are lived by the poet, often in actual life, according to the tradition; saints wear women's clothes as gopīs, Sri Ramakrishna even menstruates. The actor playing the fierce god Narasiṃha the man-lion in a mythological play, is worshiped and propitiated, lest he in a moment of possession tear the other actor (playing the demon) to pieces. The people in the audience, too, are not mere witnesses; they may join in

[70] See sections on Indian poetics in Edward C. Dimock et al., *The Literatures of India*, esp. pp. 128-29.

and partake in the poem or play through congregational singing (*bhajana*, again from the root *bhaj*); they may even become possessed by the dead poet, by a character in the play's myth, or by the god evoked in the song.[71]

4. And, as with Vedic or epic texts, the aesthetic end is subordinated to a religious end, a purpose in real life, by a special additional verse called *phalaśruti* ("a hearing of, or a recital of results"). Every unit of ten poems is closed by an eleventh, in which the poet announces himself in person in a signature verse and addresses the audience eye-to-eye, directly:

> Anyone at all
> learning these ten good verses
> out of a thousand
> made by our āḻvār,
> one of the many minions
> of our lord
> who lifted the mountain—
>
> he will be a winner
> several times over.
>
> 7.4.11

In other bhakti traditions, each verse is closed by a signature line (a *bhaṇita*), the name of the god ("the Lord of the Meeting Rivers" in Basavaṇṇa) or of the poet himself (Sūr, Kabīr).[72] Such a signature again centers the poem in a locale and a person, relating god to poet, poet to poem, and poem to audience.

5. Thus the poetry is not intended to be general, time-

[71] Folk performances also blur the distinction between possession ritual and theater. See A. K. Ramanujan, "The Relevance of Folklore for South Asian Studies," and Clifford Geertz, "Religion as a Cultural System," p. 116 on Javanese theater.

[72] See Ramanujan, *Speaking of Śiva*, Bryant, *Poems to the Child-God*, and Vaudeville, *Kabir*.

less, abstracted from the here and now, addressed to anyone who may hear, centuries from now (as Bhavabhūti the Sanskrit poet said he did)—but to a present god, or a specific audience with whom the poet shares his god, his myths, his bhakti. "Sharing" is not only the subject of the āḻvār poems but a technique as well.

Yet, in time, the poems and their very sharing create a closed community, a sect. The poems become scripture, part of a canon, to be sung only in certain temples by specialized singers; the words become passwords for a *pantha*, a way, a sect; commentaries assign esoteric meanings (the sectarian afterlives of Sūr and Kabīr are signal examples). Often the poems themselves may use a secret, often tantric, language[73]—though our āḻvār almost never does.

6. To the extent that the poetry espouses *bhāva* or "natural," "spontaneous" feeling, it tends to draw on the common stock of speech, local dialect, colloquial tones, and turns away from the standard literary language or poetic diction—though bhakti poets will use anything that is sufficiently common and will develop conventions of their own, a rhetoric of spontaneity, a complex stance of simplicity. Beginning with a first language, they may construct a second. I have spoken of these elsewhere and shall not repeat myself here.[74]

The Saint as Persona

A new kind of persona or person comes into fashion with bhakti movements: a person who flouts proprieties, refuses the education of a poet, insists that anyone

[73] See section on the "language of secrecy" (*sandhyābhāṣa*), in Ramanujan, *Speaking of Śiva*, pp. 48-49. Also note 64 above.

[74] Ramanujan, *Speaking of Śiva*, pp. 37-47.

can be a poet—for it is the Lord who sings through one (7.9.6, p. 81). The saint is no world-renouncing *sanyāsi*, no priest, no learned court poet (*pulavar*). He does not even intend to be a poet (*kavi*), and will not praise any king:

> My lord of a thousand names
>   gives and gives
>
> the fame of his giving
>   crosses all boundaries
>
> I cannot praise anyone else
>   cannot say to some paltry thing
>   of this world:
>
>   "Your hand is bounteous as the rain
>   your shoulders are strong as the mountains"
>
> I cannot tell such barefaced lies
>
> 3.9.7

The poem follows the classical *puṟam* precedent of heroic praise poetry, in which a loyal poet will not praise anyone other than his master; but the poem also rejects the classical panegyric modes ("bounteous as the rain," etc.) used in praise of kings and chieftains. The only chieftain is the Lord, and the raincloud can be metaphor only for Kṛṣṇa.

In this new type of person(a), poet and saint are one; he is a poet *because* he is a saint. In him, there is no Yeatsian conflict between sage and artist—he is not forced to choose between "perfection of the life or of the work."[75] Unlike earlier Indian poets, philosophers, sages, and so forth, whose history is rumor and anecdote, usually lost in their works, the saints are represented as full-blown personalities. Their lives and leg-

[75] From "The Choice," Yeats, p. 278.

ends surround their poetry. The saints are portrayed in biographies[76] as only the gods, demons, and holy men were in Hindu myths, and as the Buddha was in Buddhist myths. Saints' lives, the first Hindu attempts at full life-stories, are legend-like and stylized, yet unmistakably about real men and women. Both the Vaiṣṇavas and Śaivas have collections of saints' lives as part of their canon, and relate the poems to the lives. European romantics like Shelley and Chateaubriand, it has been said, lived their writings and wrote their lives, and often botched them both by doing so. But the saints, who also merged their lives and poems, became thereby exemplary. Indeed, the only true "romanticism" in Indian civilization is to be found in bhakti arts and attitudes.

As said earlier, the saints wandered over their regions, naming and singing the 108 holy places of Viṣṇu, making new guide poems, mapping man's country onto god's kingdom, weaving a network of pilgrimage centers (Tirupati, Tirumāliruñcōlai, etc.), creating "a unified field" of sacred space.

A Poetry of Connections

Throughout this essay, I have implicitly described one special feature of āḻvār poetry. This poetry of touching, sharing, seeing, the many in the one, is a poetry of connections, of continuities. It connects god, gods, and all creation; the god of myth, the god of philosophy, the

[76] The sixty-three Tamil Śaiva saints' lives were collected by Cekkiḻār in *Periyapurāṇam* (12th century), and the āḻvārs' lives in texts like *Divyasūricaritam* (12th-13th century), the *Kuruparamparai pirapāvams* (13th century). The lives were compiled not much later than the poems.

god in the temple and the god within; speaker, subject, listener; good and evil, hell and heaven, mythic *then* and poetic *now*, opposites and contraries. No distinction is made even between the workings of *karma* and the works of god, as it is in other Hindu theologies and in other kinds of bhakti (e.g., Vīraśaiva).

Dwarf,
  you confuse everyone.

But make me understand:

becoming oblivion, memory,
  heat, cold,
  all things wonderful
    and wonder itself,

becoming every act of success,
  every act of good and evil,
    and every consequence,

becoming even the weariness
  of lives,

you stand there—

and what misery you bring!

7.8.6

To see such flowing continuity as the fact of facts (even in misery) is truly to be an āḻvār, truly to be the "immersed one."

Poetically, this expresses itself in various ways, as we have seen. In closing, I will return to one striking device—the *antāti*. As said earlier, after the first poem, every poem begins with the last unit (word, segment, or phrase) of the previous one—all the 1,000 or more poems in *Tiruvāymoḻi* are linked in this way. The same form that ends and begins different poems may be used over and over in differing senses, enacting the theology of the one and the many.

The commentators speak of these poems as a *tailadhārā*, a stream of flowing oil, from vessel to vessel, from verse to verse, from mind to mind, from god to devotee. One is reminded of the emanations (*vyūha*) of Viṣṇu: "The Pāñcarātra[77] teaches a chain as it were of emanation; each emanation except the first originating from an anterior emanation; and thus the favorite image of the process has, with the Pāñcarātras, become that of one flame proceeding from another flame. Any production, up to the formation of the Egg is imagined as taking place in this way."

The very first word of Nammāḻvār's *Tiruvāymoḻi* also closes it; and it could easily be the first word of a new poem, a new cycle—a flame ready to touch another word to flame. The poem stops because poets are human, because they are mortal, because it is 3 a.m. But the poem goes on.

[77] Friedrich O. Schrader, *Introduction to the Pāñcarātra and the Ahirbudhnya Saṃhitā*, p. 35. "A widespread Vaiṣṇavite school, known as the *Pāñcarātra* ('Five Nights', of uncertain significance), gave a cosmological basis to the myths of Vāsudeva-Kṛṣṇa, by identifying him and his family with cosmic emanations, and thus building a system of evolution similar to those of the more orthodox six systems. . . . From Vāsudeva, identified with Viṣṇu, the ultimate personal godhead, developed Saṅkarṣaṇa (another name of Kṛṣṇa's brother Balarāma) at the beginning of time; this emanation was identified with *prakṛti*, or primal matter. The two produced Pradyumna (Kṛṣṇa's son) identified with *manas* or mind; thence arose Aniruddha (Kṛṣṇa's grandson) who was self-consciousness (*ahaṅkāra*). Only then did the three guṇas evolve, and with them Brahmā the demi-urge. . . . [The emanations] are not mere aspects of the divine character, but gods in their own right. . . . The gods are then simultaneously one and many. There is no question here of different levels of truth, as in Śaṅkara's system, but of an eternal paradox. The soul is one with god, but at the same time it is an individual." Basham pp. 328-29.

My lord
   who swept me away forever
      into joy that day,

made me over into himself

and sang in Tamil
his own songs
through me:

what shall I say
   to the first of things,
      flame
         standing there,

what shall I say
   to stop?

7.9.1

References

Aṇṇaṅkarācāriyār, Śrī Kāñci, Pirativāti Payaṅkaram. *Tiruvāymoḻi*. 10 vols. Kāñcīpuram: n.p., 1949-1963.

Appadurai, Arjun. "Worship and Conflict in South India: The Case of the Śrī Pārtasārati Svāmi Temple 1800-1973." Ph.D. dissertation. University of Chicago, 1976.

Ate, Lynn M. "Periyāḻvār's 'Tirumoḻi'—a Bāla Kṛṣṇa Text from the Devotional Period in Tamil Literature." Ph.D. dissertation. University of Wisconsin, 1978.

Barthes, Roland. *Elements of Semiology* (with *Writing Degree Zero*). Translated by A. Lavers and C. Smith. Boston: Beacon Press, 1968.

Basham, A. L. *The Wonder That Was India*. New York: Grove Press, 1954.

Bhattacharji, Sukumari. *The Indian Theogony: A Comparative Study of Indian Mythology from the Vedas to the Purāṇas*. Cambridge: Cambridge University Press, 1970.

Bryant, Kenneth. *Poems to the Child-God, Structures and Strategies in the Poetry of Sūrdās*. Berkeley and Los Angeles: University of California Press, 1978.

Cardona, George. "Indo-Aryan Languages." (under the head "Indo-Iranian Languages"). In the *New Encyclopedia Britannica*, 1974.

Carman, John B. *The Theology of Rāmānuja, an Essay in Interreligious Understanding*. New Haven and London: Yale University Press, 1974.

Cutler, Norman. *Consider Our Vow*. An English translation of *Tiruppāvai* and *Tiruvempāvai*. Madurai: Muttu Patippakam, 1979.

———. "The Poetry of the Tamil Saints." Ph.D. dissertation. University of Chicago, 1980.

Damodaran, G. *Ācārya Hṛdayam*. Tirupati: Tirumala Tirupati Devasthanams, 1976.

Dange, S. A. *Legends in the Mahabharata*. Delhi: Motilal Banarsidass, 1969.

Dimmitt, Cornelia and van Buitenen, J.A.B., eds. and trans. *Classical Hindu Mythology, a Reader in the Sanskrit Purāṇas*. Philadelphia: Temple University Press, 1978.

Dimock, Edward C. et al., *The Literatures of India*. Chicago: University of Chicago Press, 1974.

Dirks, Nicholas B. "Political Authority and Structural Change in Early South Indian History." *The Indian Economic and Social History Review*, vol. 13, no. 2 (April-June 1976), pp. 125-258.

Dryden, John. "The Dedication of the Aeneis." In *The Poems of John Dryden*. Edited by James Kinsley. Vol. 3. Oxford: Clarendon Press, 1958.

Dumont, Louis. "Renunciation in World Religions." In *Religion, Politics and History in India*. Paris and The Hague: Mouton & Co., 1970.

Eliade, Mircea. *Shamanism, Archaic Techniques of Ecstasy*. Translated by Willard R. Trask. Bollingen Series 76. Princeton: Princeton University Press, 1964.

———. *Yoga, Immortality, and Freedom*. Translated by Willard R. Trask. Bollingen Series 56. Princeton: Princeton University Press, 1958.

Filliozat, Jean, trans. *Le Tiruppāvai d'Āṇṭāḷ*. Pondichéry: n.p., 1972.

Geertz, Clifford. "Religion as a Cultural System." In *The Interpretation of Cultures, Selected Essays*. New York: Basic Books, 1973.

Gerow, Edwin. *Indian Poetics.* Wiesbaden: Otto Harrassowitz, 1977.

Gnanambal, K. "Srivaishnavas and Their Religious Institutions." In *Bulletin of the Anthropological Survey of India*, vol. 20, nos. 3 and 4 (July-December 1971), pp. 97 and 187.

Gonda, Jan. *Viṣṇuism and Śivaism: A Comparison.* London: Athlone Press, 1970.

Govindacarya, A. "The Astadasa-bhedas" (The Eighteen Differences). *Journal of the Royal Asiatic Society* (October 1910), pp. 1103-12.

Gros, F., trans. *Le Paripāṭal.* Pondichery: n.p., 1968.

Hardy, Friedhelm. "Ideology and Cultural Contexts of the Śrīvaiṣṇava Temple." In *The Indian Economic and Social History Review*, vol. 14, no. 1 (January-March 1977), pp. 119-51.

———. "The Tamil Veda of a Śūdra Saint" (The Śrīvaiṣṇava Interpretation of Nammāḻvār). In *Contributions to South Asian Studies I.* Edited by Gopal Krishna. Delhi: Oxford University Press, 1979.

———. "Emotional Kṛṣṇa Bhakti." Ph.D. dissertation. Oxford University, 1976.

Hart, George L., III. "The Nature of Tamil Devotion." In *Aryan and Non-Aryan in India.* Edited by Madhav N. Deshpande and Peter Hook. Ann Arbor: Michigan Papers on South and Southeast Asia, no. 14, 1979, pp. 11-33.

———. *The Poems of Ancient Tamil: Their Milieu and Their Sanskrit Counterparts.* Berkeley and Los Angeles: University of California Press, 1975.

———. *The Poets of the Tamil Anthologies.* Princeton: Princeton University Press, 1979.

Hooper, J.S.M. *Hymns of the Āḻvārs.* The Heritage of India Series. London: Oxford University Press, 1929.

Hume, R. C., trans. *The Thirteen Principal Upaniṣads.* New York: Oxford University Press, 1971.

Inden, Ronald. "Lordship and Caste in Hindu Discourse." Typescript. University of Chicago, 1980.

Ingalls, Daniel H. H. *An Anthology of Sanskrit Court Poetry.* Cambridge: Harvard University Press, 1965.

Jakobson, Roman. *Shifters, Verbal Categories, and the Russian Verb.* Cambridge, Mass., 1957.

Kailasapathy, K. *Tamil Heroic Poetry.* London: Oxford University Press, 1968.

Kumarappa, Bharatan. *The Hindu Conception of Deity as Culminating in Rāmānuja.* London: Luzac, 1934.

LaBarre, Weston. *The Ghost Dance: Origins of Religion.* Garden City, New York: Doubleday, 1970.

Lester, Robert. *Śrīvacana Bhūṣaṇa of Piḷḷai Lokācārya.* Edition with English translation. Madras: The Kuppuswamy Sastry Research Institute, 1979.

Lewis, I. M. *Ecstatic Religion, An Anthropological Study of Spirit Possession and Shamanism.* Harmondsworth: Penguin Books, 1971.

Mahalingam, T. V. *Kāñcīpuram in Early South Indian History.* Bombay: Asia Publishing House, 1969.

Mookerji, Radha Kumud. *The Gupta Empire.* 4th ed. Delhi: Motilal Banarsidass, 1969.

Nilakanta Sastri, K. A. *The Culture and History of the Tamils.* Calcutta: Firma K. L. Mukhopadhyay, 1964.

———. *Development of Religion in South India.* Madras: Orient Longmans, 1963.

———. *A History of South India.* 3d ed. Madras: Oxford University Press, 1966.

O'Flaherty, Wendy Doniger. *Hindu Myths.* Harmondsworth: Penguin Books, 1975.

———. "Inside and Outside the Mouth of God: The

Boundary between Myth and Reality." *Daedalus* (Spring 1980), pp. 93-125.

Ong, Fr. Walter J. *Interfaces of the Word*. Ithaca, New York: Cornell University Press, 1977.

Pope, G. U. *Tiruvācagam or "Sacred Utterances" of the Tamil Poet, Saint, and Sage Māṇikka-Vācagar*. Tamil text, translation. Oxford: Clarendon Press, 1900.

Purushottama Naidu, B. R. *Tiruvāymoḻi; īṭṭin tamiḻākkam*. 10 vols. 2d ed. Madras: University of Madras, 1971.

Rajagopalan, Vasudha. "The Śrī Vaiṣṇava Understanding of Bhakti and Prapatti (from the ālvārs to Vedānta Deśika)." Ph.D. dissertation. University of Bombay, 1978.

Ramanujan, A. K. *The Interior Landscape, Love Poems from a Classical Tamil Anthology*. Bloomington and London: Indiana University Press, 1967. Paperback 1975.

———. "The Relevance of Folklore for South Asian Studies." Paper presented at the Conference on South Asian Folklore: A Search for Models and Metaphors. Berkeley: University of California, February 1980.

———. *Speaking of Śiva*. Baltimore: Penguin Books, 1973.

Rao, V. N. Hari. *Kōil Oḻugu, the Chronicle of the Śrīrangam Temple, with Historical Notes*. Madras: Rochouse and Sons, 1961.

Srinivasa Raghavan, A. *Nammalvar*. Makers of Indian Literature Series. New Delhi: Sahitya Akademi, 1975.

Schrader, Friedrich O. *Introduction to the Pāñcarātra and the Ahirbudhnya Saṃhitā*. Madras: Adyar Library, 1916.

Schwartzberg, Joseph E., ed. *A Historical Atlas of South Asia*. Chicago and London: University of Chicago Press, 1978.

Singer, Milton, ed. *Krishna: Myths, Rites, and Attitudes*. Honolulu: East-West Center Press, 1966.

Staal, J. F. "Sanskrit and Sanskritization." *Journal of Asian Studies*, vol. 22, no. 3 (May 1963), pp. 261-75.

Stein, Burton. "Brahman and Peasant in Early South Indian History." *Adyar Library Bulletin*, vols. 31 and 32 (1967-68), pp. 229-269.

———, ed. "Special Number on South Indian Temples." *The Indian Economic and Social History Review*, vol. 14, no. 1 (January-March 1977).

Swami, [Shree] Purohit, and Yeats, W. B., trans. *The Ten Principal Upanishads*. London: Faber and Faber, 1937. Reprint 1975.

Thapar, Romila. *A History of India*. Vol 1. Harmondsworth: Penguin Books, 1966.

Underhill, Evelyn. *Mysticism*. New York: E. P. Dutton, 1911. Paperback 1961.

van Buitenen, J.A.B. "On the Archaism of the *Bhāgavata Purāṇa*." In Milton Singer, ed. *Krishna: Myths, Rites, and Attitudes*, pp. 22-40.

Varadachari, K. C. *Ālvārs of South India*. Bombay: Bharatiya Vidya Bhavan, 1966.

Vaudeville, Charlotte. "Evolution of Love Symbolism in Bhāgavatism." *Journal of the American Oriental Society*, vol. 82 (1962), pp. 31-40.

———. *Kabir*. Oxford: Clarendon Press, 1974.

Venkatachari, K.K.A. *The Maṇipravāḷa Literature of the Śrīvaiṣṇava Ācāryās*, 12th to 15th Century A.D. Bombay: Ananthacharya Research Institute, 1978.

Wallace, Anthony F. C. *Religion: An Anthropological View*. New York: Random House, 1966.

Yeats, W. B. *The Collected Poems of W. B. Yeats*. London: Macmillan, 1955.

Yocum, Glenn E. "Shrines, Shamanism, and Love Poetry: Elements in the Emergence of Popular Tamil Bhakti." *Journal of the American Academy of Religion*, vol. 41, no. 1 (March 1973), pp. 3-17.

———. "A Study of Māṇikkavācakar's *Tiruvācakam*: The Setting and Significance of a Tamil Devotional Text." Ph.D. dissertation. Philadelphia: University of Pennsylvania, 1976.

Young, Katherine. "Beloved Places (Ukantaruḷiṉa-nilaṅkaḷ): The Correlation of Topography and Theology in the Śrīvaiṣṇava Tradition of South India." Ph.D. dissertation. Montreal: McGill University, 1978.

Zaehner, R. C., trans. *Bhagavadgītā. With a Commentary Based on the Original Sources*. London: Oxford University Press, 1969.

Zelliott, Eleanor. "The Medieval Bhakti Movement in History: An Essay on the Literature in English." In *Hinduism: New Essays in the History of Religions*. Edited by Bardwell L. Smith. Leiden: E. J. Brill, 1976.

Zvelebil, Kamil. "The Beginnings of Bhakti in South India," *Temenos*, vol. 13 (1977), pp. 223-57.

———. *The Smile of Murugan*. Leiden: E. J. Brill, 1973.

———. *A History of Tamil Literature*. Vol. X, fasc. 1 of *A History of Indian Literature*, edited by Jan Gonda. Wiesbaden: Otto Harrassowitz, 1974.

———. *Tamil Literature*. Leiden/Cologne: E. J. Brill, 1975.

Library of Congress Cataloging in Publication Data

Nammāḻvār.
Hymns for the drowning.

(Princeton library of Asian translations)
Translation from: Tiruvāymoḻi and Tiruviruttam.
Includes bibliographical references and index.
1. Vishnu (Hindu deity)—Poetry. I. Ramanujan, A. K., 1929- II. Nammāḻvār. Tiruviruttam. English. Selections. III. Title. IV. Series.
PL4758.9.N3155A27 294.5'95 81-47151
ISBN 0-691-06492-X AACR2
ISBN 0-691-01385-3 (pbk.)